HIRED GUNS

Women in Music

Series Editor

Anna Beer
Oxford University

This book series creates a platform for ground-breaking studies which offer new insight into any and all aspects of women in music. Building on Equinox Publishing's established lists in popular music, film music and the wider industry, the series is of interest to the scholar, practitioner, and general reader.

Women in Music aims to be inclusive, seeking to publish historical and critical studies, cultural analyses, life-writing, traditional musicology and more. The series as a whole works to challenge some of the less helpful divisions in music scholarship – for example, between 'popular' and 'classical' – by welcoming submissions which range, where appropriate, across genres, eras, and disciplines. The common thread, however, remains women's lived experience, whether as individuals or groups, and/or cultural understandings of the category of 'woman'.

Almost all areas of the music industry are now waking up to women's under-representation, and not just as a historical phenomenon. Change nevertheless remains slow. Through the dissemination of the latest scholarship in the field, *Women in Music* not only celebrates and explores the often hidden contributions of specific individuals and groups, but by contributing to a richer, more complex, picture of women in music, provokes some important questions for the industry.

Published

Dora Bright: Her Life and Works in the Public Eye
Anthony Bilton

Hired Guns

Portraits of Women in Alternative Music

Amanda Kramer and Wayne Byrne

equinox

SHEFFIELD UK   BRISTOL CT

Published by Equinox Publishing Ltd

UK: Office 415, The Workstation, 15 Paternoster Row, Sheffield, South Yorkshire,
      S1 2BX
USA: ISD, 70 Enterprise Drive, Bristol, CT 06010

www.equinoxpub.com

First published 2024

British Library Cataloguing-in-Publication Data

A catalogue record for this book is available from the British Library.

ISBN-13 978 1 80050 430 1   (hardback)
         978 1 80050 431 8   (ePDF)
         978 1 80050 470 7   (ePub)

Library of Congress Cataloging-in-Publication Data
Names: Kramer, Amanda, 1961- author. | Byrne, Wayne, 1983- author.

Title: Hired guns : portraits of women in alternative music / by Amanda
   Kramer & Wayne Byrne.
Description: Sheffield, South Yorkshire ; Bristol, CT : Equinox Publishing
   Ltd, 2024. | Series: Women in music | Summary: "Hired Guns: Portraits of
   Women in Alternative Music is a look across several decades of the music
   industry through the experiences and careers of a selection of
   professional female musicians. This book is the collaboration of
   musician Amanda Kramer and author Wayne Byrne. Together they conduct
   candid interviews with their subjects and compose an insightful cultural
   and historical discourse"-- Provided by publisher.
Identifiers: LCCN 2023032380 (print) | LCCN 2023032381 (ebook) | ISBN
   9781800504301 (hardback) | ISBN 9781800504318 (pdf) | ISBN 9781800504707
   (epub)
Subjects: LCSH: Women alternative rock musicians--Biography. | Alternative
   rock musicians--Biography. | Women alternative rock
   musicians--Interviews. | Alternative rock musicians--Interviews.
Classification: LCC ML82 .K73 2024 (print) | LCC ML82 (ebook) | DDC
   781.66092/52 [B]--dc23/eng/20230807
LC record available at https://lccn.loc.gov/2023032380
LC ebook record available at https://lccn.loc.gov/2023032381

Typeset by S.J.I. Services, New Delhi, India

This book is dedicated to the memory of Julee Cruise

Contents

Acknowledgements

Amanda and Wayne would like to thank all the musicians who kindly took part in this book, as well as our editor Anna Beer. Our sincerest appreciation to Zachary Alford, Julie Panebianco, and Amy Scully for your support and assistance. And special thanks to Ene Riisna for your words of encouragement and insight.

Foreword

Jennifer Finch[1]

Ten lives.
Ten lives that beat the odds.
Ten lives well lived.

Amanda Kramer and Wayne Byrne have assembled the stories of ten exceptional musicians whose careers, influences, and experiences are contained within the alternative music universe from its commercial birth in the 1980s to the current day.

As a working musician, I have never supported media that grouped and compared musicians based on gender, race, or sexual expression. Society did that enough, and seeing it fortified by the media has always been disappointing and dismissive; however, Kramer's and Byrne's approach of 'giving the microphone' over to each musician with added context and commentary is unique and exciting. As readers, we experience the rawness and vulnerability as each musician reflects on their influences, challenges, and milestones throughout their life and career.

Media surrounding musicians has always defaulted to the fantastic, to the fabulous and convenient truths, resulting in a well-defined barrier between the reader and the subject. This approach is the mainstay of good storytelling yet sacrifices the authenticity of its subjects. As musicians, we often need to default to these devices to tell our stories in ways that ensure we can compete in the marketplace. This is especially true of women in just about any undertaking. The approach of *Hired Guns: Portraits of Women in Alternative Music* offers a distinct view of these ten musicians' lives. Instead of the usual hype one expects, Kramer and Byrne encourage their subjects to tell their stories from lived experiences so that we may better understand how they navigated the world without the added self-promotion or publicity machines that we all court for our commercial success.

I asked Amanda why she thought telling these stories this way was necessary. She and I have had many thoughtful and thought-provoking conversations on music, technology, distribution, sales, self-marketing, and more of the stuff that adds to a career. Her answer, in this case, surprised me a bit. She was thinking about how future generations of musicians would come to understand the challenges, differences, and lifestyles of their recent musician ancestors. With so much change in how we create and distribute music, she wanted these stories to be honoured as time moved on. I usually file this line of inquiry under the 'kids today don't know how good they have it' category. Yet, coming from Kramer, I know it is a genuine effort to help us all understand each other, our ordinary and extraordinary circumstances, and how as individuals we remain connected, even when it feels like we are alone. As I read through this collection, I was compelled to compare and contrast each story with a universal (and a little generational) perspective. I asked:

> *Did they have support from their families?*
> *Was music a key feature in their family homes?*
> *How did counterculture versus mainstream media influence their work?*
> *Did they feel part of a community?*
> *Did they find guidance from mentors or role models?*
> *Was there a music programme in their schools?*

Of course, there is never a concrete formula, especially in our post-postmodern age; each musician's story is unique. Looking for a practical blueprint to guide us is useless.

However, within each tale, a common thread is to be teased: *Steadfastness.* That unique energy stitches together these musicians' lives through the fabric of time and space. To read this collection is not simply to read about ten random lives of recording and touring musicians but ten impactful lives of dedicated souls who beat the odds through their unique blending of resilience and effort.

These are ten authentic lives, authentic lives well lived.

Note

1. Jennifer Finch is an American visual artist and musician.

Introduction

Amanda Kramer

This book is constructed around a series of ten interviews conducted by Wayne and me. All the musicians chosen were either those I have personally known for many years, or they were those whose careers I was curious about, as they have been on my radar since the early 1980s. Of course, I have met many other brilliant musicians along the way, but we decided on limiting the interviews to these ten specific artists so that we could present their stories with the depth and substance that we feel they deserve. We hope that we have succeeded, and that the reader will find their lives as inspiring as we do.

1 Gail Ann Dorsey

As is common in this book and in many an historical account of popular music, the East and West Coast cultural capitals of New York City and Los Angeles (and London if we are talking Europe) appear as the backdrop and birthplaces of momentous musical movements. But across the first half of the twentieth century, the Great Migration brought millions of African Americans from the Southern United States to the West, Midwest, and Northeast of the country, and it was in the rural and urban environs in which these displaced people settled and built their communities that, over several decades, jazz and gospel music would emerge as thriving examples of American art. Midwestern and other non-coastal cities benefitted culturally from the Migration; consider the effect and influence that importers of the Delta Blues such as Muddy Waters and Buddy Guy had on Chicago music. Another town ripe for renewed interest on the wave of incomers and their attendant art was Philadelphia. That city in particular saw a marked increase in its Black population upon the Migration, and it would prove a natural home for impending musical styles which, in the 1940s and 1950s, were then blended in the city's cross-cultural melting pot which resulted in the amalgamated form known as rhythm and blues (the original R&B), an era-defining genre distinct in its dynamic dance rhythms and blues melodies. The subsequent merging of this popular style with country music created the template for what would become the greatest musical phenomenon of the twentieth century: rock'n'roll. Bill Haley would herald the emergence of this form, and along with his band The Saddlemen (later, His Comets) he increasingly eschewed the country elements in favour of a contemporary urban R&B style. With this, his was an acceptable white face for a music rooted in the Black neighbourhoods west of downtown. Of course, Haley was not alone as a purveyor of gospel, country, rhythm and blues in the neat package of rock'n'roll, for he would soon be joined by Memphis son, Elvis Presley. But rock'n'roll was not racially exclusive, as soon to join Haley and Presley on the national airwaves were African American pioneers of authentic R&B, such as Fats Domino (out of Louisiana), Jackie Wilson (of Michigan), Little Richard (of Georgia), Etta James (of Los Angeles), and Chuck Berry (of St. Louis).

Dick Clark's local Philadelphia radio programme and later national television showcase *American Bandstand* would spotlight Philly natives such as Chubby Checker, Charlie Gracie, Fabian, and Frankie Avalon. The hit songs and great records coming out of the city in the 1950s made sure that it would forever be associated with the birth of rock'n'roll, but popular musical styles are as nebulous as a teenager's musical tastes. When Dick Clark moved his iconic operation out of Philadelphia to the heady lights of Los Angeles in 1964, it was somewhat symbolic of the changing face of Philadelphia's music culture.

By the mid-1960s, under the influence of the counterculture and its various ideological interests, rock'n'roll evolved and drew upon elements of folk, baroque, progressive, and psychedelia, as well as incorporating less-polished production techniques in forming new versions of rock music. Philadelphia was one of many American cities which built its own scene of underground rock with local acts including (early Todd Rundgren group) Nazz, The American Dream (whose debut album was also Rundgren's first production work), and Mandrake Memorial. As the 1960s rolled on and the conflict in Vietnam raged, the counterculture engaged in fierce ideological warfare on the battlefields of college campuses and the media; but the music played on, often heralding changing times, often invigorating a youth movement losing hope for a new society. The children of the sixties were tuning in and dropping out to Jimi Hendrix, Jefferson Airplane, The Grateful Dead, Crosby, Stills, Nash & Young, and the like.

One of those children who paid close attention to the radio waves blasting out from WIP-610 AM was Gail Ann Dorsey. A West Philadelphia native born in 1962, Gail was the youngest of five kids, a 'surprise baby' in her own words, meaning she had the benefit of older siblings and their attendant record collection to peruse and inherit. 'My siblings were a lot older than me – I had a sister and three brothers', Gail affirms.

> They had a lot of records in the house but none of my siblings pursued a music career, although one of my brothers dabbled in it, and he still does now in his seventies in Atlanta. My siblings' record collection was such a mixture of stuff, everything from Earth, Wind & Fire to Cream to The O'Jays, and my mother's favourite – Gladys Knight and the Pips. But there was a lot of Jimi Hendrix records around, as well as Chicago, Terry Kath, Neil Young, Grand Funk Railroad, and groups like Rare Earth and a San Francisco-area band called Cold Blood who were amazing, they had this great singer called Lydia Pense. They were one of those rock-soul bands, kind of funky, jazzy, and they had a horn section and everything, so it was like power-funk-rock from the 1970s. They didn't release

many records but the stuff they did was incredible. The guitar in that really appealed to me, as did Eric Clapton's solos in Cream and Neil Young's guitar solos, which were always really out there.

Back in 1960s and 1970s America, most people got their music from only one source: the radio. Albums were expensive and people had to save money to buy releases from their favourite artists. This was before the music industry decided to divide up artists into different genres for the sake of marketing, so one was exposed to various musical styles all coming from the same station. It was this kind of eclectic programming approach that Gail benefitted from, as she explains:

> I grew up in a Black neighbourhood in West Philly, where a lot of the kids there were listening to the likes of Sly Stone and the funky stuff. But I always had my Olivia Newton-John and Joni Mitchell records going. And Heart. I loved the Wilson sisters. But it was like this secret thing. So, I got a little bit scorned from the other kids because of what I was listening to. I was a big AM radio fan, it was WIP-610 AM in Philly, and one reason I loved it was because of the guitar stuff, and because you would also have The Carpenters, Dionne Warwick, Burt Bacharach, and Olivia Newton-John, whose voice is just like heaven to me. My mother always had the AM radio on in the kitchen, it was just this thing that was always on, and now I do the same; it's a comfort thing, I guess. But that's the music I liked: I had my Barbra Streisand, my Karen Carpenter, my Dionne, my Olivia. Philly was a great place to be, but it was tough. It is probably much the same now in terms of segregation, but back then it was super segregated to the point where you really couldn't cross boundaries. There were areas that you really shouldn't go to.

With the sound of music abounding the Dorsey domicile, it wasn't long before young Gail would endeavour to add to the strains. She received her first musical instrument on her ninth birthday when she was gifted an acoustic guitar from her godmother. Three years later her brother would hand her an electric guitar, which felt like a licence to the young music enthusiast to go and create her own noise. Along with two other similarly aged neighbourhood kids, a couple of boys from across the street who respectively played bass and drums, Gail would initiate the inception of her very first musical group. Taking on the local school auditoriums and playing for anyone who would listen to them at block parties and on porches, Gail and co. belted out Grand Funk Railroad covers for the assembly.

'We would play very simple rock stuff, because I wasn't that great yet, and neither were the guys', she admits.

I really loved Mark Farner's guitar in Grand Funk Railroad, they had those riffs that I would learn by just playing along to, that basic kind of stuff. Also, I loved Tony Maiden of Rufus. I learned guitar from listening to those two players, Tony and Mark, a lot – I wore those records out! Then for more chordal things I was trying to learn Joni Mitchell songs, but I could never get them right because I realised that she used fucked-up tunings; I was struggling to figure out how she played her things, so I was like, 'oh, I give up'. But me and those guys were just getting out and playing on the porch all day, all summer, for whoever wanted to watch us. We would do block parties and have people in the neighbourhood join in.

While Gail has become known as one of the world's preeminent session and touring bass players, she admits that the guitar is first and foremost the instrument she maintains most affection for.

The guitar was my first love, and it is still my main instrument, I still love it. But I could never get as good on the guitar as quickly as I did on the bass, for some reason. There was a time when I was much better on the guitar, but I feel I need to get more proficient again. I haven't been playing much guitar lately because I've been writing more on the keyboard; not that I'm a keyboard player but I can map stuff out on it. The bass was an accident for me, I never wanted to be a bass player.

But a bass player she became, by necessity. At fourteen and with school out for summer, Gail sought a summer job. Too young to flip burgers at the local McDonald's, or any greasy spoon, the only available option was also the most ideal: a Top 40 bar band. She would soon find out that there was already a proliferation of guitarists out there, but they were all looking for bass players. Scanning the billboard of pinned 3x5 index cards at the Sam Goody in downtown Philadelphia, notice after notice sought every kind of player other than the omnipresent six-stringer. She had to change tack.

I wanted to make some money that summer, but I was too young to have a proper job, you had to be at least sixteen, and I didn't want to do that anyway; I just said, 'I want to be in a band'. But I had to find a band that was working, so I went to the Sam Goody because they had a big billboard on which people would advertise that they were looking for musicians, so that's where I went to look for work. I can still see the board to this day, tonnes of cards that said, 'guitarist seeks drummer', 'guitarist seeks bass player', and so on. Quite a few people needed a bass player or a keyboard player; everybody was a guitar player looking for another instrumentalist for their band. Back then the telephone numbers had letters at the beginning which told you what neighbourhood it was, and there was this one card which had my mom's neighbourhood on it that said, 'Guitarist seeks bass player for Top 40 band. Summer work'. It must have been kismet. They were a working band and had summer work lined up.

Gail took the number down, but she didn't have a bass. The Dorsey household was not an affluent one; when the family patriarch passed away in 1968, he left a wife with five mouths to feed. By the time Gail was a teenager and requiring the accoutrements of such, including a new bass guitar, there was only a modest household income on which her and her mother lived.

When I was a teenager it was just me and my mom, because my siblings were out of the house at that stage. I was the only kid left and we were living on Social Security, which meant my mom didn't have a whole lot of extra money to be buying instruments for me. But if I needed something she was very supportive, God bless her. So, her and our neighbour would go to the suburbs and serve dinner to rich people or clean somebody's house for a little extra money. I said to my mom that I'm going to go audition for this band, but I don't have a bass, and I asked her, 'if I get the job could you get me a bass?' She said, 'yeah, sure...' because she didn't think I was going to get the job! The guys across the street used to rehearse in my mother's basement, which meant their drums and bass were always there; so, when they'd go home, I would go down at night and put Grand Funk or Led Zeppelin on and try to play the drums or bass along to those records. So, I learned a little bit of drums and a little bit of bass along the way. I thought, 'the bass is easy, it's only one note at a time, so maybe I could get this job'.

Gail continues,

My sister's best friend, Bettie, had a boyfriend who owned a Rickenbacker bass and he let me borrow it for the audition, but my mom said, 'you're not going to some stranger's house by yourself!' So, Bettie, who was eighteen or twenty by this point, came with me. We went to the audition, rang the doorbell and a Black guy opened the door, and I was surprised because the card said 'we're going to play The Stones, Zeppelin, Elvin Bishop...' whatever was Top 40 at the time, so I was thinking it was going to be a white guy because of the rock stuff that he had mentioned. But it was this little black guy named Jay Medley who was an incredible guitar player and who ended up becoming like a family member to me. He was four years older than me and has unfortunately passed away, so he was eighteen at the time I auditioned for him. He had studied music, but I had no lessons. I taught myself, so I couldn't read music and I still can't. I don't know much about theory; I get the idea about theory, but I don't know how to apply it to what I'm doing because it doesn't make any sense to me, Music theory is a foreign language to me, really. But Jay had studied guitar and had all the chops and he taught me all the fret names. He became a teacher to me. The funny thing is that when he opened the door he thought Bettie was the one who was there to audition; so he was like, 'wow!' because she was really pretty – she was half-black, half Japanese. He assumed I was the little sister tagging along, so he was thinking, 'score!' But then he found out that he was actually auditioning me! For the audition we played Elvin Bishop's 'Fooled Around and Fell in Love' which I sang and played at the same time, and he didn't know I could sing. So, I got the job, and my mother bought me this Epiphone bass. But it was difficult because I was underage for some of the venues, so he made a deal with some of the venue owners that I would stay in the back. The owners would say, 'you go out there and do what you need to do for those thirty minutes but before you start and as soon as you're finished you stay out back, because if someone walks in and sees you, we could lose our license'. So, there was this kind of danger to it where I would go and play the set and then run out back to hide and eat French Fries. We played throughout that summer, and I made some money, but it was only for that summer; after that, when I was sixteen, I started playing my own music with a band I was in with two older guys. That's when I started to write songs, so I was bringing my original stuff to that band.

When it came to further her academic studies, Gail pursued her first love: cinema. Moving to the West Coast to enrol in California Institute of the Arts, Gail studied Film with the view to becoming a screenwriter and director. She had begun to seriously indulge in her passion whilst in high school, making Super 8 movies with her friends to screen on her own home projector.

'Those little, short films and a screenplay that I wrote are what got me into Cal Arts on a full scholarship when I was fifteen or sixteen', she affirms.

I just love film, and that's why I ended up going to college to study it, because I was serious about getting into it professionally. Film had been my serious interest other than music as a teenager. I was really into movies and screenwriting. It was something that had been there forever. It started with TV because I was too little to go to the movies by myself, especially to see the things that I wanted to see. But it was just something organic, watching movies a lot, as much as I could.

Cal Arts was originally conceived as a merger between Chouhinard Art Institute and Los Angeles Conservatory of Music, but it became most famous for its animation division after Walt Disney developed the school in the early 1960s as a factory for animators whom he could pull out and put to work for his Disney film studio. Given its conservatory origins, the college was also a highly regarded campus for its music programme which had assembled a faculty of notable people from the jazz world, including Charlie Haden, the pioneering bass player of the Ornette Coleman Quartet. Having players of such esteem teaching there gave the college a certain allure to budding musicians. But jazz as a cultural and artistic form initially appeared on Gail's radar through her keen interest in cinema before she discovered some crucial albums that encouraged her interest in the genre. Gail recalls that:

> Cal Arts has five arts disciplines, it's got Dance, Theatre, Music, Art, and Film, which is divided into animation and live action, and I was in the latter. But while I was there, I met a bunch of musicians who were playing a lot of jazz and reggae, things that I didn't listen to before. I didn't have any jazz records or anything, what I knew about jazz was from soundtrack stuff. My real introduction to jazz was by Joni Mitchell, mainly through the album that she did with Charles Mingus [1979's *Mingus*]; that's the one that got me listening to jazz.

The seismic shift from the grand orchestral compositions of Hollywood's Golden Age to the minimalist jazz scores in the late 1950s and early 1960s with the emergence of the American New Wave led to the genre becoming a mainstream Hollywood concern that even the Oscars couldn't ignore. Miles Davis's improvised score to Louis Malle's *Elevator to the Gallows* (1958) redefined the film soundtrack and its relationship to the motion picture. Duke Ellington would elaborate on this style with his score for Otto Preminger's *Anatomy of a Murder* (1959), and then with Martin Ritt's *Paris Blues* (1961) he would make history as the first African American nominated for a Best Music Academy Award. Throughout the 1960s and 1970s, jazz would dominate the mainstream Hollywood score, and would introduce a new generation of countercultural film lovers to this vibrant and unpredictable genre of music. Gail was one of many young film lovers enthralled by this exciting marriage of music and moving image:

> Films were so good in the '70s, they have such a wide variety of music in them; the soundtracks were brilliant. I liked the fact that music was such a big part of cinema. Listening to music would

give me ideas for stories that could be made into movies; I would put on some music and think of stories and visual ideas of what could go along with it. Usually, it is the other way around – a film is made and then you get people to put music to it – but for me music inspired ideas for things that I could write into a screenplay … a story that would fit the music.

Unfortunately for Gail, and for the film industry, she would not pursue her interest in the discipline any further than the first semester of her second year on campus. Surrounded by the boorish behaviour of male classmates and intimidated by the experience of those who had already gleaned years of experience at Hollywood studios and on professional film sets, Gail sought solace in the burgeoning music scene bubbling under the radar at Cal Arts. She recalls,

I realised that in the Class of 1980, I was the only female, and a lot of the people in the course had already been working in the film industry; they had come from different places like Brazil and Germany, and there was somebody from New York, but they were all older and they all had the practical experience of having worked on a TV show, or on a film, or whatever. They were more experienced than me and had done all this for real before, they already knew how to load a 16mm camera; but we all had to go through the same course, and I was really intimidated. Those guys were shits, total male chauvinist shits. I'm sure there's more women in the classes now, so there's more people to stand up for you, but back then I was the only girl in the class, and I was living away from home, so that was tough. I had to find my way.

She continues,

I met people from the other schools and there was a place called Mom's Café where we hung out to eat and listen to music; people would bring their guitars and play there, and I had gone to Cal Arts without my guitar so I went to the Saugus Swap Meet and bought a $30 Mexican guitar and I would bring that down to Mom's and start jamming. And I just started thinking, 'nah, I gotta play music', because the film thing wasn't working, between those kinds of guys in the class and with the time it takes to get some kind of feedback in the world of film, the reward of it can take years. That may be okay for some, but I don't have that personality, I need a more immediate response to what I'm doing, which is why I like touring so much; even though it might be hard on the road there is nothing like being on stage and being in the moment and having that connection with the audience. For me, it is even better than being in the studio. But in film, if I'm the screenwriter then I'm the very first person in the chain, then you've got to sell the script, find the producer, find the actors, and so on, and by the time you're finished with all that you might not even recognise your own story. In theory I knew it was 'a tough business', but to live it was a whole other thing. Some of those guys would sell their mother to make it, but I don't want anything that much to step on somebody else to get it. So, I figured out that was not the business for me. I love movies but unless I had the money to just make them the way I would want to do it, then it's not for me. I left the school after the first semester of the second year; so around '82 I dropped out, went to New York City and tried to cut some demos and get a record deal.

Hollywood's loss is music's gain. Gail and her Cal Arts friend, Pete, a native of London, England, arrived in New York City with nothing but a keyboard and a dream. Gail says,

Pete was in the design school at Cal Arts and he also came from a musical background; he played keyboards, and we decided to drop out of college together in order to move to New York to 'get back to music'. So, we drove across country and got a sublet. He would work in restaurants – as you do when you're young and you go for it – and I found work in a place called The Record Factory on West 8th Street, that was my first job when we got to the city. It was this little two-floor record store, all vinyl and cassettes, CDs were about to come in, but then Tower Records opened up and put us out of business. After that I worked uptown in a Sam Goody on 51st and 6th Avenue, right across from Radio City Music Hall. I think it's a bank now, but they had CDs there because I remember stocking the shelves with these long plastic packages that you had to break apart to get the CDs out. Vinyl was still big too. I remember the day I opened the box for Michael Jackson's *Thriller* to stock the shelves before we opened, and then once we opened the doors I went back to the register and every single person I served bought a copy of that record, you couldn't keep it in the store! It was odd because somebody could be buying an album of Bach or Pavarotti or Tom Jones, but they would also have a copy of *Thriller*. It was so bizarre! That record was so popular that everybody had to have it.

Whilst Gail toiled by day making ends meet in the hardscrabble of life in NYC, she did get to experience the full electro-shock cultural experience of the downtown arts scene that thrived underground, just before it bubbled over into the mainstream.

She recalls,

> I liked to free-float around with my friends. We used to go to The Garage, but I would mainly stick to private parties more than going out to clubs, because I was still underage. I didn't turn 21 until I was in London, and I never had a fake ID, so I didn't bother with any of that. I mainly went to these more underground parties with my friend Adele Bertei, who is still one of my best friends; she did that film *Born in Flames* [directed by Lizzie Borden] and she was friends with [No Wave filmmakers] Beth and Scott B, who had made the movie *Vortex*. So, I would go to these parties with Adele and hang out with people like that. I remember going to a loft that they said was Basquiat's loft and Madonna was there; I'll never forget it, she was there waving around her 12-inch saying, 'I'm going to be famous! I've got this record that is coming out next week.' And we were like, 'who is this woman?!' Those are the kinds of parties I went to; I never got into hard drugs or that kind of scene – although I did have my coke days, but that is a horrible drug, so I preferred to smoke weed. Weed keeps me calm and helps me focus; when I don't smoke, I get a little dark. But I'm not a stoner, I don't collapse onto the couch with a box of cereal or anything, it is a natural, medicinal aid for me.

Meanwhile, Gail and Pete were shopping their 8-Track demos around town to little success; it would become evident that record companies had pre-conceived notions of what a Black artist should look and sound like – an aesthetic that Gail didn't, nor wouldn't, subscribe to. Eventually, the pair decided it best to hop across the pond to Pete's hometown of London where they continued to persevere for success.

> I had written a bunch of demos with Pete; we had this thing going where I think we were trying to be like the Eurythmics or something. I was writing songs and he was playing keyboard. But in New York, no matter where I would shop my demos, they wouldn't get it. I'm not really an R&B/Soul kind of artist, I love that music but it's not my forte – it just isn't what I gravitate towards. But I suddenly realised that to be a Black woman in the music industry – or a Black artist in general – that is what they expected you to do. When you did something different, they just didn't get it. Pete didn't ever want to get caught living in New York without a visa and take the chance of never being allowed back again, so he decided to go home, and I was like, 'take me with you!' I said maybe if I go to London and bring my demos with me something might happen over there. We were such good friends, and I met his mom when she was in New

York. They were kind of a well-off family, and I went to England in August of 1983 and lived with them for about six months. After that I lived in Brixton. I lived in South London, in Clapham North, for the rest of my time there after I bought a flat with the money that I received for my record deal. I love South London, though I'd hardly recognise it now. I went to Brixton a while ago and I was like, 'what?!' it was so gentrified. When I was there it was Eddy Grant *Electric Avenue* time.

Once firmly ensconced in the musical nightlife of London in the mid-1980s, Gail wouldn't return to the US for four years, only then to promote her debut solo album, *The Corporate World*. And while she missed out on the tumult of the Reagan years, she would live on the doorstep of his political peer, the Iron Lady Maggie Thatcher. Despite the cultural and social upheaval of the period, it was a time which proved ideal for Gail to enter the London musical landscape and make a name for herself amongst the burgeoning indie underground.

Pete's family were living in Finchley, right in Margaret Thatcher's constituency, and it was the height of her craziness when I arrived. But it was the best time to be there for music. I feel like a lot of my career was because I was in the right place at the right time. Someone asked me the other day about what advice I would give to people starting out and after thinking about it I said, 'just put yourself out there', because I've met musicians along the way who don't want to go on tour and things like that. But you must make a sacrifice, sometimes you might have to sacrifice a relationship, or a family, or an animal, your car, or your house, but you've got to go out there. Looking back on it, I'm probably not as adventurous now as I was when I was nineteen, because back then I was ready to go. I had nothing to lose. I was like, 'yeah, I'll move to London, I'll figure out a way to stay, I'll sleep on the couch, I just need to play'. If you really want something, you focus on getting it. I was always willing to go somewhere and meet somebody.

Within her first couple of years in London, Gail proceeded to get a taste of professional musical life, gaining experience as a studio player for the likes of Boy George and Donny Osmond, booking demo sessions and showcase gigs for labels like Virgin, all the while honing her skills on the road with various acts. She recalls,

I did my first tour with a band called the Trashing Doves, they were two brothers, Ken and Brian Foreman, and two friends of theirs. They were a big signing by Chris Briggs at A&M. They were great songwriters, but it just didn't take off for some reason. I did a tour and two albums with them, and I loved it, they were so talented. But that was my first 'tour'. We did a club tour in the US and then we opened for Alison Moyet in Europe.

Soon enough, she found a receptive label for her demos in the form of Sire Records, and so she signed to WEA (Warner Music Group) in the UK. 'It was Seymour Stein and this girl named Shirley Divers who signed me; Shirley was British but based in New York, she worked for Seymour for years and since has passed away from cancer, but she was really my champion there'.

The resulting album, *The Corporate World*, was an assured debut and one of immense promise for an interesting career to follow, even if not in the way one expected it to unfold. Released in Europe in 1988, with the US following in 1989, it is a truly eclectic album, certainly not one that could easily be pigeonholed into the iconography of a certain genre. Across ten tracks, the album features a fine blend of sophisti-pop, rock, and R&B, on which considerable contributions from Eric Clapton and Gang of Four's chief sonic architect, Andy Gill, appear. Recorded in studios as far apart as Bath, Islington, Camden, Hollywood, and New York City, the album's pristine production by Nathan East gives the smoother tracks an extra radio-friendly sheen whilst his own bass chops provide the heavier and funkier tracks a tight and lively rhythm alongside the two powerhouse drummers Steve Ferrone (Average White Band, Mick Jagger, Steve Winwood, Cyndi Lauper) and Gavin Harrison (King Crimson, Lisa Stansfield, Black, Lene Lovich); truly a rhythm section to behold. Evidently, having East on board helped bring in the best of the best in building Gail's artistic statement of intent.

Nathan was one of my bass idols. Steve Ferrone was on drums, and he is still my buddy to this day, we did another album together a few years ago for Daphne Guinness. It was Nathan's idea to bring in Eric Clapton because he was playing with Eric a lot at that time. However, Andy Gill was my A&R guy's idea. His name was Colin Barlow; he was young and into bands like Gang of Four, so he said to me, 'you really should use Andy Gill from Gang of Four!' and I was up for it. I love unique guitar players like Andy, so I said, 'does Andy want to do that?' and he did. Andy's guitar is the very first thing you hear on the album, wailing in on the track 'Corporate World'. The first note! We ended up working together a lot. God rest his soul.

Despite a couple of choice cuts released as singles, including 'Wasted Country' and 'Where is Your Love?' the album still made an inauspicious debut appearance by missing out on the British charts. Unfortunately, once again Gail would come up against corporate bureaucracy and ignorance, facing an endless cycle of meetings with marketing executives and other besuited types whose idea of Black artists fit a narrow mould from which they could shape the next Whitney Houston. Egregiously, the US label even insisted on cosmetic changes to Gail's album which would lose any thematic subtlety that lay within the grooves of the record.

Gail says,

> The US label made me change the cover because it didn't indicate what it was. I already had a cover on which I'm wearing this suit that is a map of the world that a woman from Belgium handmade for me, and I'm holding *The Financial Times*, that was my idea for the cover. But because it was more of a rock record, or rock-pop, they put me in a leather jacket against a white background and a guitar, and I'm like, 'does that tell you what the music is like?!' But that's what I was up against with the US guys, but in the UK and Europe they were like, 'cool!' I didn't get that thing of, 'well, you're Black but the album is not really gospel'. They didn't know how to market it, and that was an issue that primarily came up in the United States, it never came up anywhere else in the world. Shirley [Divers] was always in my corner, but it was such a fight because of things like having to change the cover, and then when I went to the US, I had to do all these stops at the Warner Bros. offices across the country, talking to people in boardrooms who were like, 'we're not sure how to market this ... it's a Black woman, but the music isn't soul ...' I went to Warner Bros. in LA, one in Philly, then to Sire, and so on, all to meet the people who didn't know what to do with me, so it was a waste of time. They don't even know what they want, so how could I give them what they want when they don't know what it is. I wouldn't even know how to change. I just do what I want to do. It is possible to do your own thing. Grace Jones was doing her own thing. When I saw her for the first time that made me think, 'see, you can be a Black woman and do something completely unique!' Nobody does what Grace Jones does. Ultimately, *Corporate World* did fairly well, it didn't do *too* badly. Then I went on a European tour for the album and that was pretty successful, playing the Paradiso in Amsterdam, the Ancienne Belgique in Brussels, Grosse Freiheit in Hamburg and selling shows out. I've always had a good audience in France too. All the European markets did better than the UK. And then it came time to do the second record for which I had these songs but then this new thing came along, which was, 'the single! The single!' And at that point I was like, 'this sucks!' so I asked my lawyer how I could get out of the record deal because I didn't want to do this. Then we found a technicality in the contract where it said that as long as we deliver

the album the label still has to pay us, it doesn't say they have to like it. I had delivered the second album and then I asked to get out of the contract and wanted to be paid for the delivery of the album. So, we got some money on that after we won on the technicality, which allowed me to walk away from that label.

Gail continues,

I just became disillusioned with the record companies and now I know you don't need them very much. I took time off after *The Corporate World* and lived in Amsterdam for a year. I have some good friends there and I began to write a little more while trying to figure out what I wanted to do. I was able to decide what I wanted to do next, and my thought was to work for other people because I just wanted to play. I was playing with bands around London, they would be bands who had record deals but who never really took off, or with bands that would be doing showcases; any opportunity to play really, I didn't care what it was. I wanted to just keep playing for other people because I loved playing all this different kind of music, from Trashing Doves to Gang of Four to Louise Goffin's band. I was just enjoying being part of the ensemble. Ever since I was a kid all I wanted to do was to play in a band. Maybe I'll have a band that is just my band someday, but I like playing for other people. I enjoy going from different artists to different artists, you meet a new family each time. I've been lucky to be able to go from one great artist to another, and I've never had to call anybody for a job, one thing would always lead to another; somebody would see me playing and then they would call me to go work with them.

And the girl played on. She began picking up steam as a noted session player in the early 1990s, touring and recording with an eclectic variety of artists including the Hollywood-based alternative trio, Concrete Blonde. Gail appeared on the band's 1990 commercial breakthrough album *Bloodletting*, and can be heard on the record's ultimate track, 'Tomorrow, Wendy'.

I love Johnette [Napolitano]. She was good friends with Ken Foreman of the Trashing Doves and we did some gigs together with Concrete Blonde, so that's how I met those guys. She saw me play and asked me if I wanted to come and play on 'Tomorrow, Wendy'. I have a platinum record of that from Canada, it is the only disc that I have from someone I played with. Concrete Blonde was a great band, I used to go see them play in Amsterdam and all kinds of places whenever I could.

Another major step forward in Gail's career came when inveterate post-punks Gang of Four reconvened after breaking up in the aftermath of their 1983 tour in support of their fourth album, *Hard*. Anglo-American musician Sara Lee had been playing bass with the band up to that point, having replaced previous players Dave Allen and Busta 'Cherry' Jones. Lee not only elevated the funkiness of the band's sound but brought a melodic voice which contrasted nicely with the edgier elements of their sound. But by the time guitarist Andy Gill and singer Jon Lee decided to reunite for 1991 album *Mall*, Sara Lee was busy at work with The B-52s. Her absence could only be glaring and a huge void to fill, but that is when Gill remembered Gail; having performed on her debut album as well as on some further unreleased material, he knew she would come armed not only with considerable chops on her instrument but with a remarkable voice. And so, the Gang invited Gail into the fold for the recording of their fifth album. With the vapid, over-produced chart rock of the late 1980s stumbling into irrelevance as the dour grunge genre consumed the alternative music scene of the early 1990s, things were bleak in the alt-rock realm, but Gang of Four's *Mall* stood out as a breath of fresh air. Not conforming to any fashionable music culture of the time, the album is tightly rhythmic and songful in the band's own distinctly unique manner. It largely eschews the pop-flavoured production techniques of previous album *Hard* in favour of returning the band to the more uncompromising angular sound of their earliest compositions, songs that bristle with some of the rawest tones of their career, such as the single 'Cadillac', as well as some quieter, melodic moments as found on 'Motel', which features some rare acoustic guitar from Gill. Only rarely does *Mall* revisit their former proclivity for the synth-laden disco funk of erstwhile albums (as heard on 'Don't Fix What Ain't Broke'). Gail's deep, low-end bass is often staccato, frequently pulsating, yet always subtle and tasteful, making hers a stunningly fitting addition to the band's line-up. Touring duties would soon follow, again at the request of nominal bandleader Gill. Gang of Four took to the road, performing across Europe and the US on an impressively eclectic bill that also included Public Enemy and Sisters of Mercy. It was on this tour that Gail got to realize a goal that she had harboured since working the cash register at Sam Goody's and daydreaming at the legendary venue right across the road.

> Andy had said to come and do *Mall*, so I did. Then after recording the album, he asked me if I would tour the record with them, so I was like, 'yeah, why not?' Then we went and did some shows in the US and Europe throughout '91, we did all the sheds in the States. Gang of Four was actually the first band that I got to play Radio City Music Hall with, we played there on that tour. I remember being in tears because I said to Andy, 'you know, I used to work right across the street at Sam Goody's and I would sit there at the till looking out at the Radio City marquee every day and think, "one

day I'm going to play there!'" And they were the ones who got me there for the first time.

Gail's tenure with Gang of Four led to further associations with Gill, as when it came time to for him to produce INXS frontman Michael Hutchence's 1995 solo album, released posthumously in 1999 and on which Gill brought Gail in to provide backing vocals on tracks such as 'Flesh and Blood' and 'Slide Away'. Working with such an unorthodox player as Gill was an opportunity for Gail to collaborate with one of the truly original players to come out of the British punk scene and who would go on to influence generations of players to come with his avant-garde sound and aesthetic. 'Andy was so unique', she applauds,

> he had all these little gadgets and that rhythmic thing that he could do with the sound of the guitar was so original. He wasn't a technical player with noodling chops, those are often my least favourite types of players, but Andy's playing had personality. Okay, Brian May is a noodling kind of player, but he has a distinctive sound and personality as well as the chops; and then you have Jeff Beck, but that's because he's Jeff Beck and he does things with the guitar that nobody understands how to do. Andy was one of those original kinds of players who are really rare and exciting. And his style was funky too. It was hard to define, it was punky, but it wasn't purely post-punk; it had a flavour of that, but it had this funky thing happening along with this avant-garde sonic element that made Andy a true original.

While Gail was building her portfolio of work with other artists, the pull of another solo record brought her to Chris Blackwell and his Island Records, who signed Gail to record and release her sophomore album, after having previously failed in their bid to secure a record deal with her first time around for *The Corporate World*. Despite the impeccable catalogue of albums and enviable roster of artists on their books, Island would prove another unfortunate experience for Gail, who once again faced boardroom indifference after corporate politics changed Island's operations when its parent labels Polydor and Polygram intervened to shake things up.

Gail recalls,

> Chris Blackwell was one of the bidders for my first record, along with Virgin and Warner Bros. It was like serendipity. I had a manager in London called Guy Davies and he partnered with John Scher, who was repping me in New York, and it was while John was on holiday in the Bahamas that he saw Chris Blackwell, who asked John what I was doing. Chris told John how much he really

wanted to sign me, so John told him that I just left Warner Bros. and Chris said, 'I want to grab her!' So, Chris calls me and I signed with Island. Working with Chris was the total opposite of Warner Bros., he was just like, 'do your thing! I'll be the executive producer, but I want you to do whatever you want to do'. He didn't have a query about, 'where's the single?', he was great. As soon as we finished the record, we mixed it at his studio down in Miami; he had a studio set up in a hotel, like a mixing suite, and one night I was in there mixing until one o'clock in the morning and Grace Jones walked in! She came in and listened to one of my songs and I nearly died! Chris did wonders with her, and they were still close friends. That's why I should have picked Island for my first record – they had The B-52s, Grace Jones, Bob Marley – but then not long after the record was finished Chris left Island. Polydor took it over and he left, he was like, 'I'm no longer the kingpin here'. So, he didn't help me out from that point on. It became Polydor and my second album, *Rude Blue*, came out and I went to New York again, where I was told, 'oh you're just another one of Chris's eccentric signings and we don't really know what to do with you'. So, I'm like, 'fine, whatever', and they put out around 3,000 copies of that record. It's a very rare record, people are still trying to get it. After that I just said I don't want to deal with record labels anymore, I'm just going to go on and keep playing for other people.

Fortunately for Gail, it wasn't long before she would be back on the road doing what she loves, as word had been spreading throughout the British music scene since the release of *The Corporate World* heralded her as a talent that many would look to work with. A seasonal social meeting with Tears for Fears co-frontman Roland Orzabal led to the next phase of her career as a session musician.

My friend Adele [Bertei] had gotten the gig to sing with Tears for Fears on the tour for *Songs from the Big Chair*, and I went to a Christmas party at Roland's house with Adele at the end of that tour. I met Roland there and he knew my solo work. Most people in London knew my record; it wasn't a hit, but I had a presence, so he knew that I played bass and sang. And not long after that he had a fight with Curt and then he wrote the album *Elemental* which was something to do with the demise of their relationship. So, Roland called me and said, 'Curt's out and I've kept the name Tears for Fears. I've done this album *Elemental* and I'm going to take it on tour, so would you be interested in taking Curt's place and playing bass?' I was like, 'yeah, cool!' And the band was incredible, the musicians were from a band called Wire Train who were this LA group that Roland found that included Jeff Trott, Brian MacLeod, and Jebin Bruni. Al Griffiths was a high school friend of Roland's who was a really good guitar player and who helped him write a lot of stuff on *Elemental*. It was those guys and me, and I was doing songs like 'Woman in Chains'.

As soon as the band finished touring *Elemental*, they headed straight for the studio to record Tears for Fears' fifth album (and second without Curt Smith), *Raoul and the Kings of Spain* at the Record Plant in Los Angeles. Wasting no time or talent, Orzabal planned on returning to his own home studio in Bath as soon as *Raoul* was in the can with the view to writing and developing a third solo record with Gail. Orzabal had previously steered Tears for Fears collaborator Oleta Adams ('Woman in Chains') to solo prominence when he produced (along with David Bascombe) her third album, *Circle of One*, and had similar designs on Gail.

'Roland just had a big hit with Oleta Adams' *Circle of Love* album which he produced, so he had in mind to do the same thing with me', she admits.

It wasn't a record deal or anything, but we had a production thing together. After we came off the tour for *Elemental* we went into the studio in LA and recorded the next Tears for Fears album, *Raoul and the Kings of Spain*. We did that when the big earthquake happened in California, the power kept cutting off in the studio and everything, but after recording that album we went back to Roland's house in Bath to work on the material for this solo record that he was going to produce for me. We were writing songs and we had Brian MacLeod come over from LA; we all lived in the house, played tennis, and hung out. We'd go into the studio every day, put the DAT machine on and just jam and come up with stuff.

But sometimes the best of plans and intentions get interrupted and side-tracked, as when David Bowie calls on the phone looking for you. As Gail recalls,

One day, Roland's wife Caroline came across to the studio looking for me. I could see her coming through the glass doors, she was running over with the baby in her arms, and she looked pale. Then she slides the door open and says, 'David Bowie was just on the phone for Gail!' I was like, 'what?!' She said, 'yeah, I picked up the phone in the kitchen and it was David Bowie. He's going to call the studio in five minutes, I gave him the number!' I was sure it was somebody playing a joke, but then the phone rang, and I go into the office to take the call and I say, 'who is this?' And it was Bowie! He spoke to my manager and tracked me down to Roland's house.

At that point I had one foot in Woodstock, I was just moving back to New York in '94, but Bowie said, 'Where are you, love? I'm going to be doing this tour with Nine Inch Nails in the fall [of '95] and this is the band I'm putting together, it has Carlos Alomar, Reeves Gabrels...' I'm thinking, 'oh my god!' and I told him I'm in Bath writing songs with Roland. He said, 'well, I only need you for six weeks and you can go back to your record after that'. When I went back into the room Roland and Caroline were sitting there waiting and were like, 'well...?' And I said, 'he is doing this tour for six weeks and he wants me to join his band'. So, I'm just looking at Roland and he says, 'well, of course you have to go, it's fucking David Bowie!' I went, and I never made it back to Bath. But I have to say I really enjoyed working with Roland, I felt that he really got me, and we were coming up with some really good stuff. There were a couple of things that ended up on my last solo record which were things we developed during the writing session in Bath. But I went on the Bowie thing for six weeks and then as soon as it was over it was like, 'now we're going to do this...' I was back in Woodstock, and he was in New York, so it was all go.

Thus began Gail's two-decade association with David Bowie, as the six-week US leg of the Outside Tour (which featured support from Nine Inch Nails) would lead directly into the recording of the *Earthling* album, cementing their collaborative relationship in the process. *Earthling* would feature the same stripped-down configuration of musicians that formed the singer's backing band on the Outside Tour, which included Bowie's old Tin Machine cohort, Reeves Gabrels. 'Reeves was probably my favourite of the guitar players that I worked with', Gail affirms.

He is another one with that gift on the guitar. You don't hear it so much when he is playing with The Cure, even though they are a great band, but I don't think I've ever been on stage with a player who was so exciting, I never knew *what* was going to come out of that damn guitar – he would ring it out and make it scream, he just had such unbelievable *control* over the instrument. That is the thing I liked about guitar as a kid, that I was able to create a sound that expressed an emotion that I could not express in any other way. I could hear those emotions in the guitar, and it made me think, 'that is exactly how I feel!' It's so hard to explain but Reeves was like that night after night, he would be playing a solo and I would be getting chills. He can play any kind of style and it's effortless.

When her schedule permitted, Gail continued to perform with other acts between her Bowie engagements, and one particularly memorable detour saw her roam around in some rather kitsch attire as she went to the wild planet of The B-52s. Gail exclaims,

> They were my neighbours upstate, Kate [Pierson] was there, and Keith [Strickland] was up there for a while too, but he moved on. Kate and I used to do a lot of stuff locally; we had a band called The Chanteuse Club with another singer and a piano player and we would do these gigs upstate which were a lot of fun. Then at one point Cindy Wilson left to have a baby and they asked me to step in. I did sub for Sara [Lee] one time when Charley Drayton was on drums, which was so wonderful; it was for some corporate event or other, but then I did few shows with them when Cindy was off having a baby and I really enjoyed it… 'just put on a wig and have a blast!' Singing songs such as 'Love Shack' was like karaoke, and Kate's my friend, so it was a load of fun. I think their first two records are genius, especially that album *Wild Planet*, with those songs 'Devil in My Car' and 'Quiche Lorraine'. Just brilliant. They are one of my top favourite bands of all time, they are so original, there's never been another band like them.

Back on planet earth with the Starman, Gail continued to tour with Bowie, embarking on worldwide promotional treks for the *Hours* and *Heathen* albums, as well as undertaking the biggest road journey of his career with A Reality Tour. Only the singer's 2004 heart attack brought the show to a premature stop. Throughout these tours, Gail's striking stage presence could be as commanding as that of her iconic boss; they shared a distinct chemistry which became a celebrated feature of the concerts – their showstopping rendition of Queen and Bowie's 1981 duet 'Under Pressure', with Gail assuming Freddie Mercury's vocal parts, could be a highlight on any given night. Bowie retired from touring in 2006, but Gail and he would collaborate again, with her next major contribution to the Bowie oeuvre being on the recording of his 2013 album *The Next Day*. The project was shrouded in secrecy, owing to Bowie's distrust of internet vulture culture in which everything is scrutinized, even before official release. Only Gail's friend Sara Lee knew of the impending studio adventure, the subsequent sessions of which Gail soon found to be memorably unorthodox. As far as everyone else was concerned, she was working on a moneyed Swedish project of little note, when in fact Gail was heading down to an inconspicuous SoHo recording studio, The Magic Shop, to lay down David Bowie's 25th studio album.

> *The Next Day* was a very special album to work on because it was that one that nobody knew was happening; it came out after he had

his heart attack and after almost ten years of not doing anything. Suddenly, he called up and said he wanted to do this album, and everybody had to sign this thing which said we had to be quiet about it. It was such a secret project that at the end of the day David would go around and take up everybody's charts and bring them home so nothing could be leaked. At that point when he was starting *The Next Day* he said, 'I'm so sick of the internet and things leaking out every five minutes'. Somehow someone gets hold of a track and it's put out on the internet, and it means you can't create in private anymore. There was a time when you didn't know that an artist was creating an album and then all of a sudden there's a new record out for you to listen to. And because he hadn't released an album in so long, I knew he was feeling like, 'the internet is full of people talking shit all the time, speculating, and asking, "what's the new record going to be like?" and often they will already have an opinion about it before they ever hear it'. He had an idea of how things were going to turn with music and the internet, and he wanted to avoid all of that.

Since Bowie's death, the artist's spirit has been kept alive by myriad tribute shows and gatherings in honour of his legendary legacy, though it is not something that Gail feels terribly comfortable engaging in, with the odd exception...

The first few shows we did after he died felt almost like a funeral in a way, just getting together to send him off and play some music. But I'm not really down with those tribute bands, and there are a few of those around. However, there is one tribute that we have been doing in New York, at The Cutting Room, on his birthday and it features Donny McCaslin and the bassist and drummer from Blackstar – Tim Lefebvre and Mark Giuliana – and the guitarists change sometimes but it's usually always people who have an association with Bowie in some capacity – we had Gerry Leonard this year, and we also had [singer] Catherine Russell and [percussionist] Everett Bradley join us. Being that it's The Cutting Room it is intimate and this year we did three nights which were sold out. It's just so, so good, to me that's the best tribute to see. I'm not real big on the Bowie conventions either, but I recently did one with Carlos Alomar – whom I *loved* playing with – and it was fun. It was the first one I ever did and Donny McCaslin, who was the sax player on *Blackstar*, was also there; he was one of the last people to work with Bowie. Woody Woodmansey who was on the *Spiders from Mars* record was there as well. Even though I usually steer clear of those things, I must admit, it was fun...

It was crazy to lose David, it was like the whole world changed after he died. It's like post-Bowie the world started going crazy, something weird happened. Bowie has been the most amazing person, he single-handedly changed my professional life; in fact, I don't even like to say 'professional life' because he changed my life, period. Music is my life; it's what I live to do. I feel like I've been given a gift to be able to do that, so to squander that would be a horrible thing to do. I think back to myself as a kid in Philly and remember what I wanted to do with myself musically, which was to have my own band, something like Rufus and Chaka Khan. I never thought I would be good enough to play in someone else's band or to play with an artist like Bowie, because even in those days the musicians who played with people like Frank Zappa and David Bowie were famous in their own right, because if you were playing with people like that it meant you were *really good*. So, I never imagined I would be part of one of those kinds of bands.

Gail's modesty is not affected for the sake of humility; she is more than aware that it is rare for a session musician of her standing not to be formally trained and proficient in music theory. Gail cannot sightread or write music; she is intuitive rather than theoretical. Getting gigs has never been an issue for someone of her natural skill and her ability to play by ear, but stepping into Bowie's playground felt like stepping onto a whole other level of performance, where she would be working with lauded orchestrators such as Tony Visconti (as she did on Bowie's album *The Next Day*) and musicians of classical prowess.

My thinking was, 'I'm never going to go back to music school to learn all that shit, so I'm never going to play for Bowie or Zappa or someone like that'. But working with Tony was amazing, he is a brilliant producer, especially with the orchestrations, and he definitely did have charts for some of that stuff, and he could put a chart in front of me if he wanted to, but … he would have to explain it to me as best he could, or play it, or let me hear it on a demo. As long as I could hear it, maybe played on a piano or have someone show me it, then I can pick it up and I will play whatever they want. David was pretty open about things; on *Earthling* he was just like, 'go for it!' They had a basic idea for that stuff, but I pretty much had a free hand with my bass on it.

Some artists, however, are more particular than others when it comes to how their hired guns replicate their recorded output when it comes to the live arena. Lenny Kravitz was one such artist whose fingerprints are quite literally on most instruments that are heard on his records; and being a multi-instrumentalist of some versatility and certainty, he expects his chosen musicians to replicate precisely the notes and the tones as those on the original polished recording, right down to dictating which instruments his musicians play. Gail was happy to oblige when she was asked to join Kravitz's belated tour in support of his 2011 album, *Black and White America*, even if it did mean leaving her most beloved bass behind.

> I didn't use Marylin, my favourite bass, which is a Stingray that I have played on everybody else's work except for Lenny. I make a point of using that on every job if I can. That one goes with me, with my ashes. But Lenny likes it to sound like it is on the record. He is one of those people who could live in the studio for the rest of his life if he could. He loves making stuff perfect, but then when we go on the road, he is always chasing that, which can be stressful because you're never going to get that. He wants the fills in the same places that they are on the record, he wants the tone to be exactly right. It was the only gig in my whole career on which I didn't play any of my own basses. He had a '61 jazz bass that he bought for me when I started that gig because it has a certain tone; I had a '59 p-bass and some other things but they just didn't have the tone that he wanted and I get it, that's fine. I am there to serve the song and the artist's vision. I did get to play a Stingray on a couple of things. Ernie Ball had just reissued the classic Stingray, so it was just old school enough. They gave me one of those and I was able to play that with Lenny on certain things where he had some slap bass. I could use the Stingray for those songs.

After getting caught up in the Bowie whirlwind, Gail never had the chance to finish the mooted album that she and Roland Orzabal had begun in earnest back in Bath. However, some songs destined for that project did end up on her third solo release, *I Used to Be*, which is a 2004 collection of various songs written at different stages of her life and career.

> I called it *I Used to Be* because some of the songs on it were demos from when I was a teenager that I re-did; the album was made of songs from that time up to the point where I was in my life when I recorded it. It was Sara Lee who made me do it, she is the Executive Producer of that record, she was like, 'you've got a bunch of songs lying around, just go and do them and I'll help you!' We just got our good friends and some local players from Woodstock – of which there are many – and we went into Allair Studios, which is where the Bowie album *Heathen* was recorded. It was a private place in Shokan, New York which was located at the top of a mountain with this 360-degree view of the reservoir, it was just stunning. It was really hard to get up there in winter because there was only one

road up to it. It was owned by this wealthy guy, Randall Wallace, who also owns a huge guitar collection. The majority of the tracking was done live in the big room there at Allair and a little bit of it was done in Saugerties. Tony Visconti had worked there before; it was him who dragged Bowie up there to record *Heathen* in 2002. Bowie used to laugh at me for living in Woodstock, he would say, 'what are you doing living up here with all these old pot smoking hippies?' And I would say, 'because I *am* an old pot smoking hippie!' He would tease me for living up there, and then he ended up getting a place up there after *Heathen* – after he recorded at Allair and saw the view he said, 'ah, now I know why you live up here with these pot smoking hippies!' …

Some of the songs on *I Used to Be*, such as 'Philadelphia', was something that I originally recorded on my 4-track Tascam when I nineteen. I was really adept at working with tape, I was really more prolific when I was using that stuff. But then it became obsolete, and I started to work with Logic on the computer, but I just don't feel as creative when I'm working with that. I know what is happening and what I need to do in the analog world but working with the computers just stumped me. The digital way of recording makes it easier in some respect, I can do what I want with it but it's not the same; I feel it has hindered me a little bit. It's not that I don't like technology, I *do* like it, I just prefer doing things with actual machinery. And tape, of course, sounded a certain way. It was like being in Film school, where I learned how to edit on a Steenbeck; you were in the dark room with white gloves on and all the reels of film there in front of you. It was so exciting, but now it's like, 'I'll just do it on an iPhone'. I'm thinking I might do what Bruce Springsteen did with *Nebraska* and go get my Tascam out of the closet, then everybody will go, 'oh wow!'

Gail brought *I Used to Be* to the stage with a sparse, solo acoustic set of the album's tracks, after which she would sell CDs. Bowie allowed her to sell the CD as part of the merchandising on the A Reality tour, which helped to recoup a big chunk of the money she spent on the project, and internet download sales of some of the tracks still bring in the occasional royalty. It was during this jaunt of promoting *I Used to Be*, after a show at the Beacon Theatre in New York City supporting her friend Ani DiFranco, that Gail took a rare moment of professional privilege to secure some VIP passes to meet her childhood hero, Olivia Newton-John, who was performing with the Baltimore Symphony in that very city. It was an opportunity too good to pass up and turned out to be a serendipitous decision that would lead to one of the biggest personal and professional achievements of her life.

I did something that I hardly ever do, something I've only ever done twice: I asked my manager if he would call her manager and get me a meet and greet. I *never* do that, but I did it for Heart, and I did it for Olivia Newton-John. She was my childhood favourite; I just think she has the most beautiful voice. If the angels would sing to me that's the voice that I imagine they would have. It is just a very familiar, wonderful voice of my childhood. I wanted to go and see her live. I had never seen her in-person before. So, my manager arranged that, and they said, 'she will meet you before the show because she has to catch a plane right afterwards and won't be hanging around'. I was like, 'oh my god!' So, I booked a hotel room and got in my Honda Element and drove down to Baltimore. I was so excited! I think I even brought a vinyl album for her to sign. So, I got there, they took me into a room, and the tour manager said she will be coming down in a minute and she will take a picture with me. I was beside myself. I was so nervous! And then in walks her guitar player and bass player. Her guitar player was also her musical director, a guy named Andy Timmons, and he's an amazing guitarist from Dallas. Lee Hendricks was the bass player. The two of them came into the room before Olivia came in and they said, 'we heard you were here and we wanted to meet you, we're huge Bowie fans!' So, they were excited to meet *me*, and I don't know what to think because Olivia Newton-John is on her way, so I'm freaking out. I really was! So, they talked to me for a while and they were really cool, then Olivia comes in and I take a picture with her, which is on my wall at home. Olivia was one of the sweetest, most amazing people I have ever met; she was so kind, and normal.

Elated with that night's concert and armed with a photographic memento of her meeting as a reminder of that fleeting but meaningful moment, Gail went back home and thought nothing much else of her conversation with Andy and Lee, until, that is, some years later she received a private message from Andy Timmons on MySpace. As the Musical Director of an upcoming Newton-John tour, this was less a social missive and more of a pressing professional one that required an imminent reply.

It was around 2009 and I get this message from Andy Timmons where he's like, 'hey, it's Andy Timmons! Do you remember me? I'm Olivia Newton-John's guitar player'. And I'm like, 'yeah, of course I remember you!' And he said, 'well, Lee is going to go work with Eric Church and we've got some gigs coming up, so I was wondering if you wanted to come and play bass. It's only for a couple of weeks at a time'. I remember reading the message and I was jumping up and down with excitement. And then I called him and said, 'Andy,

I can't read music!' And he said, 'none of us are reading music! Just come on out here, you can do this'. And I was just like, 'I don't know', because songs like 'Sam', 'Making a Good Thing Better', and all those complicated 70s songs with all the chord changes and everything ... I can't play all that Leland Sklar stuff. But Andy just reassured me and said, 'of course you can!' So, I thought, 'I have to try it, this is my idol, I've got to *try* it at least!' The rehearsal was in Nashville. I went there to this big hangar, and I learned the set. The funny thing was I knew those bass parts, and I knew those songs, like the back of my hand. I didn't have to learn them; I already knew them so well; I knew exactly where the bass did a fill, I knew when the guitar or the horn would come in, and the strings, and so on. I didn't even have to make my own little chart, which I do sometimes. We did three medleys, there was a medley from the '80s, there was a medley of country music, and there was a main medley at the end and all the other songs in-between, and she sang every one of those songs in the original key. I was worried that they would want to play the songs in different keys, because I knew how to play them in the key that they're in on the record. Bowie changed the keys all the time, a lot of singers do, but she sang everything in the same key as it is on the records, and she was no spring chicken at the time.

Gail continues,

I always dreamed of playing with Olivia Newton-John, but in my mind, I knew that job would mean having to read the music, there's no way you could just pick it up. I figured her band would be from Nashville and would be these incredible players, so there's no way I'm ever going to play with her. But I did and it was the best gig of my life. Truly, the greatest moment of it all was when I got to play with the one person that I did dream of playing with my whole life, Olivia Newton-John. The last show I did with her was in Adelaide at a gay festival, and we had the Adelaide Symphony with us, and the last song was 'I Honestly Love You', which opens with the strings and the cellos were playing behind me, and I swear to God I felt like I was levitating. I was out of body at that point. And then that voice comes in [*sings*], 'maybe I hang around here a little more than I should...' I'm hearing all of this through my in-ear monitors, and it was just the most pivotal moment. I could have died right then. That moment was just incredible. Olivia was my pinnacle. I don't think anything can or will ever match that.

2 Clare Kenny

Throughout the past forty years, Clare Kenny has brought her significant bass grooves into the studio and onto several tours for artists such as Sinead O'Connor, Indigo Girls, Shakespears Sister, Aztec Camera, Orange Juice, and Amazulu. The latter band, a quintet of politically charged females who had arisen from the anarchy-fuelled ashes of the punk milieu of the late 1970s, was Clare's first taste of life on the road as a professional musician. And what a trial by fire it would be! It was a life contrary to that which her classical musical education would suggest that she was poised to pursue. Born to an Irish family living in Birkenhead as part of the Liverpool-Merseyside diaspora, the Kenny clan later moved to Wales, where Clare would be attuned to her parents' party pieces which consisted of folksongs and Irish ballads. Raised in a musically nourishing household, it was only a matter of time before Clare and her sisters were encouraged into classical training. While the Kenny sisters took up the piano, Clare found that taking lessons from an 86-year-old piano teacher wasn't for her, and so she began to study classical guitar, meaning it wouldn't be long before she was learning musical theory via the six-string. Clare and her sisters would be the first generation of the Kenny family to have the opportunity to go to college and whilst studying in Plymouth she had figured that her interest in environmental sciences would be a sensible career path to pursue. But then boys and bass came before academia. 'I decided to take a year off because I was so sick of school', Clare confirms,

> I was hanging out with friends down there and got involved in bands. I was playing electric guitar at first in a punk band and then I got interested in the bass after I was asked to play it for a band whose bassist had let them down a few times. So, I picked it up and learned the songs as they weren't that difficult, and I thought 'this is where I belong!' Because I love reggae, the bass really chose

me. From then on, I was a bass player. I went to London with my boyfriend's band, and we were going to conquer the world.

While global domination proved elusive, London's calling proved fortuitous regardless. Arriving in the city in 1979, Clare and her boyfriend split up and she would soon find a new musical home, and employment, at the Islington pub, the Hope and Anchor. The bar was the heart of the London music scene, providing a stage for much of the emerging alternative music culture that was simmering and soon to explode in filth and fury. Clare recalls,

> I was renting a room for ten quid while I worked in the Hope and Anchor. I fell into that job, and it was a lucky break as that pub was so much a part of the London music scene. It was a great time for music in London. Everybody from everywhere came down to London and that's part of the reason why there was a lot going on. It's hard not to think about London today as being quite sterile in comparison – I'm sure there's a little hot-spot of young people doing their thing, but I'm not immersed in that, so I don't know. And I had the option of working extra hours in a cocktail bar across the road, while I was signing on! It was very easy, but for young musicians now it certainly isn't. How would they afford it?! There are these colleges now – The British Institute of Music and so on – and it just makes you think, 'You don't need to go to college to be in a band!' You do tend to think that there must be some individualism and rebellion about being a musician (or artist) don't you? When punk came along with ska, reggae and 'people's music' it kind of blew a hole in the kind of class system which had dictated what was 'good' on narrow, boring, safe lines. Punk put an end to all that in music. Maybe the objectives have changed now, maybe it's all about writing film soundtracks. I don't know what those kids are expecting because it seems they're all after fame and fortune; that has always been a lottery ticket, and it's the parents paying for it. Punk allowed young people to realise that they didn't need to get a degree or spend years playing classical guitar in order to have a go. An amazing flow of ideas, creativity and rebellion, collaboration, poetry, politics was unleashed. Everybody that I worked with, and myself included, had punk to thank for getting us off the ground. Times have changed!

For many aspiring musicians in the late 1970s it was all-eyes-on-London, which was heralding a profound marriage of rich multicultural, multiracial identities that was parlayed into something musically vibrant and original. With influences as varied as American garage rock and Caribbean reggae, the roots of both could be heard in many of the emerging acts from the punk and post-punk music movements. These acts represented the first generation of musicians coming from a background of colonization; the children of Caribbean emigres who landed in England throughout the 1950s and 1960s to escape socio-economic hardships and look for work. They also imported elements of their own West Indies culture to the London music scenes and in doing so laid the groundwork for thriving underground scenes to develop and engender an influential artistic cross-pollination.

Indeed, the visibility of and cultural engagement with Caribbean music was initially engendered in large part because of the crucial November 1972 release of the film *The Harder They Come*, which starred and showcased the music of Jamaican reggae star Jimmy Cliff. This and the English embrace of Bob Marley and The Wailers were significant markers in this pop-cultural upheaval. Both Cliff and Marley were signed by Island Records and were supported greatly by the record company's chief, Chris Blackwell, who co-produced Marley's 1973 album *To Catch a Fire*. The British public took notice of the record thanks to its fusion of rock and reggae elements and a busy UK promotional tour which took them to the BBC television studios to film slots for various music shows, all broadening Marley's appeal. This was the era of much middle-class navel-gazing of the posturing prog predilection (Pink Floyd, Genesis, Yes, and their ilk), but within the next four years the grassroots do-it-yourself aesthetic and ethic of the punk scene emerged to blow the doors off the old boys' club, allowing disillusioned working-class Brits and the descendants of Caribbean immigrants to join forces in picking up their instruments to have their moment on stage and have their voice heard in the popular cultural realm. Indeed, the intoxicatingly exotic sounds of Bob Marley, Jimmy Cliff, and Desmond Dekker, along with the anybody-can-play-it attitude of punk, proved influential to many youths looking to music for a way out of the doldrums of late 1970s Britain, and the music industry reacted as it would to any potentially commercial revolution: with great enthusiasm and expectation of monetary returns. But it wasn't at the expense of the genuine political expression of the acts they signed and promoted. It was a heady, activist time, and music festivals such as Rock Against Racism reflected the rhetoric of the artists and their audience. Out of this socially motivated, politically aware musical culture arose a striking mix of bands, poets, and writers, among them Steel Pulse, Aswad, Lynton Kwesi Johnson, Benjamin Zephaniah, roots and reggae artists who performed around the same club circuit that also functioned as the arena of the punk movement.

The result of such musical integration can be heard in the work of bands such as The Police, Gang of Four, The Specials, Public Image Ltd, The English Beat, and Big Audio Dynamite, all of whom hit the charts and introduced dub and reggae to a lot of listeners who might not otherwise have discovered that kind of music. However, it was perhaps The Clash who most effectively and visibly incorporated the musical styles of the imported Caribbean culture into their fiery brand of British rock'n'roll. Theirs was a musical melange that heralded the fact that punk had aligned itself with reggae, and which could be heard in earnest on albums such as *London Calling, Sandinista*, and *Combat Rock*. Another group emerged and harnessed the disparate generic elements of punk, ska, dub, reggae, and pop to successful effect; it was Clare's first significant band, Amazulu. They originated as an all-female act comprised of Sharon Bailey, Lesley Beach, Rose Miner, and Debbie Dredd, but this incarnation split and the version of Amazulu with which the British music scene would become familiar soon emerged. Vocalist Anne Marie Ruddock replaced Miner, drummer John Nardo Bailey replaced Dredd, and along came Clare. Clare recalls,

> I met Amazulu in the Hope and Anchor actually. It was my night off but my friend who I shared a house with was working so I popped in on my way to somewhere else and they were there. They had just split up some previous incarnation that had gone wrong and hopped in a taxi and ended up at the Hope and Anchor wondering where the hell they were going to get a bass player from. My friend said, 'Oh, I know a bass player!' So, when I arrived I was introduced to them and they arranged an audition. That's how I joined the band. In the right place at the right time or what! The likes of The Specials and The Belle Stars were our icons, they had already established themselves by the time we came along in the early '80s. We started out as very rootsy and very serious, we were mixed race, we wrote songs about Greenham Common; we did have some memorable times together though, such as being thrown into prison in Finland!

The details of such might seem better suited to a book entitled *Bands Banged Up Abroad*, but such is the comical absurdity of the situation that it must be amusingly relayed here, highlighting the unpredictable realities of touring life. Amazulu had played a festival show in Sweden when they embarked to Finland and the unfortunate incident occurred. With alcohol consumption being restricted in Scandinavia of 1983, it meant that binge-drinking abounded whenever access to it became unfettered. As such, the ferry to Finland became a booze cruise that resulted in a culture clash of criminal proportions. Clare recalls,

> We were on the ferry to Finland and having a good time at the bar, having a bit of a dance, but there was a lot of very drunk people around and we were a bit concerned at the racism that we were hearing being bandied about. We had our Duty-Free bags with us and the security on board had been watching us very carefully because we were unlike anything they had seen before: three

Rastas, one white girl with locks, and the rest of us with spiky hair. They were convinced we were going to be stealing from the bar and would follow us around. They gave us a warning about not drinking from our Duty-Free bottle, but our promoter was pouring it under the table and when somebody saw him doing that all Hell was let loose. We were thrown about behind the bar, attacked by these stewards, they sprayed some of us with tear gas, and there was a Finnish Dog-handlers Club on board who volunteered their dogs, these Alsatians, to control us. Our sound man got thrown down the stairs by a bunch of thugs who were drinking in the bar. One of the passengers in the lounge area pulled our percussionist's hair out, so she had a bald patch for months. We were all thrown into the brig and, outrageously, the three Black members of the band were handcuffed all night. We were going to throw the book at them the next day but what happened was we were taken down to the police station where we got booked and then taken to the local prison where they kept us behind bars for two weeks. You couldn't make it up, it was insane! We'd heard that the same thing happened the previous week to one of the big rock bands of the time, they had gotten into a similar fight on this same ferry. That crossing allowed people to get really pissed because they could drink as much as they wanted on it. But after their scuffle, the band, which was a heavy metal band or something like that, had their tour manager open a briefcase and produce ten grand. And so, all charges were dropped. But we didn't have that sort of money to buy our way out of it. But the funny thing was when we were in the prison, our song 'Cairo' was going up and up the charts in Finland and it was being played on the radio. So, all the prisoners would be hanging out of the windows with their radios rattling the bars when our song came on.

A court case ensued in their absence as the band was permitted to fly home to England. However, Clare would scrutinize every subsequent tour itinerary for any potential Finnish concert dates. The nervous musician would have to sidle up to the tour manager and whisper, 'oh no, not Finland!' Luckily for her, it was always cancelled, except for one European jaunt with Sinead O'Connor which required Clare's presence in the country. 'I would be thinking, "Am I going to have anything nasty sitting on my record?"' she admits, 'but thankfully nothing happened when we got there – though I did hyperventilate a bit going through border control'.

If a positive outcome arose of the controversy, it was that Amazulu were noticed by David Bowie, who invited them to support him on his 'Serious Moonlight' tour at the Hammersmith Odeon in 1983. Indeed, it would be hard to imagine any present-day bands getting up to such anarchic mischief. Standard industry practice is for Top 40 acts to be groomed by A&R men for commercial success, and those who rebel will usually pay the price. Even New York City's artistically credible punk artists fell into the Village groover trap, which was devoid of any political context. Meanwhile, Amazulu's profile was rising thanks to hit singles such as 'Too Good to Be Forgotten', their cameo on the irreverent BBC comedy, *The Young Ones*, and promotional appearances on *Top of the Pops*, but things changed when the dark influence of narcotics shook the band's stability to its core.

'I had a great time in Amazulu until the drugs kicked in', Clare admits.

> Things changed when certain factions started breaking up the trust between the band, the drugs obviously didn't help! Back in the '80s heroin was everywhere, it was so cheap, and everyone was dabbling in everything that was going but in the band some of us got into it in a bad way and it was covered up and denied for years; one of the band members came out of the woods around six years ago, after having gone down a very dark rabbit hole. We always used to write together but then band members began not showing up; to cover up they would make up stories about their car breaking down, or they would turn up two days late for a session at the studio and then start getting crazy about how they were going to explain it. So, the rot had set in, and we were just keeping the wheels on in the hope that we might get over it or have a significant hit. But would that have helped?! It never happened anyway, and in the end the record company decided to cut their losses. They offered Annie, our singer, to go with one or two other people in the band and get rid of the rest of us. It was terribly sad. I remain friends with three of the people now, two of which were in my part of the group which got thrown aside. One of the girls went and got rehab and is now in Arizona, playing djembe and is doing great. I reconnected with Annie about two years ago over the phone – it was lovely to speak to her after more than 30 years!

In the dying days of Amazulu, Clare made acquaintance with a drummer named Zeke Manyika, who had played on albums by The Style Council, The The, and Orange Juice. It was this connection which led to Clare taking some much-needed respite from the slow-motion implosion of Amazulu to play on several albums and tours with other artists. Manyika introduced the bassist to Orange Juice frontman Edwyn Collins, who duly invited her into the studio to record the band's eponymous third album and hit the road with them to promote it. But despite being offered official band membership by Collins, she wasn't quite ready to leave the day job.

> It is one of my great regrets, although you can't regret anything, that Edwyn asked me to join the band, but I didn't because I was a bit

loyal to Amazulu. I was mixing the two up, doing both at the same time, and even though I loved Edwyn and loved his music, I just couldn't quite say, 'bye, girls! I'm leaving now!' I did continue working with Edwyn though. I played on the *Gorgeous George* album, and I toured with him as his bass player whenever he needed me. It was through an Edwyn connection that I met Pete Walsh of The Apartments around the same time as well. I played on *The Evening Visits...and Stays for Years* album which came out in 1985. So, I was constantly working within the Scottish indie world and the London indie world.

When Clare ultimately left Amazulu she joined the band of country singer, Hank Wangford, the satirical alter ego of erstwhile gynaecologist Dr Sam Hutt. 'That was a very theatrical outfit', Clare says,

Hank was quite the character and had this motley crew of band members who were all great players. There is a great groove and swing to country music, and we really channelled that style and brought in bluegrass elements, and we played Nashville, which was a thrill. I also met one of my oldest friends, Kath, in that band. We did a lot of festivals, we toured Ireland many times, and me and Kath got to go to Bulgaria to do a TV show with Hank for Channel 4. It was great.

After a few years with The Hank Wangford Band, Clare would find further work with another old friend of Edwyn Collins, Roddy Frame, the singer and songwriter of the socially conscious Scottish indie rock group, Aztec Camera. By 1987 they were no longer a band but essentially a solo project under the complete control of Frame, who crafted a fine commercial pop record in *Love*, from which the hit single 'Somewhere in My Heart' was released. The track, now a perennial 1980s compilation favourite, was slickly made by pop and hip-hop producer, Michael Jonzun, and elevated Aztec Camera's profile considerably. Poised for major mainstream success but having little interest in replicating the song's heavily processed, radio-friendly engineering, the following album, *Stray*, would revert to a more modest production style, but the 1991 world tour mounted in support of the album would be of a scale that Clare had never experienced before. Clare was still with Hank Wangford at the time that the audition for Aztec Camera came up, but as much as she loved being part of that band it was time for her to move on at that point. And so, she went for it and got it. 'I was so excited', Clare enthuses.

What an amazing experience – I had never done touring on that scale. That was an opportunity to see touring on a completely different level; there was Catering, there was Wardrobe, Tour buses, trucks full of gear; it was a production of twenty-nine people or something like that. And apart from the catering woman, I was the only other female there. I did find that as the months went on, I was missing female company quite a lot. The guys were lovely, but I would have to take myself off to health spas, have my hair groomed, get massages, and have some essential oils time.

Clare's desire for female company in a musical milieu which is largely populated by men would be fulfilled within the next few years as she would embark on several projects which featured many well-travelled women of the road. At this point, Clare was working with The Wolfgang Press, a post-punk band whom the bassist loved; they were signed to 4AD though had absolutely no money. Unfortunately, brilliance and credibility don't pay the bills, and Clare found herself financially struggling until the fortunate moment she received a call from Steve Blackwell, manager of Shakespears Sister, the pop-goth act that began life as a solo project for ex-Bananarama singer Siobhan Fahey after she left the chart-topping trio. However, Fahey was soon joined by American songwriter, Marcella Detroit, an inspired collaboration as the ensuing 1992 album *Hormonally Yours* brought great success and attention from yielding the massive hit single, 'Stay', as well as several other top ten singles. With their popularity at its peak, it was time to take it on the road, a considerable jaunt that Clare couldn't resist. Clare recalls,

> They were looking for a good cross-section of men and women musicians to audition, so I got the call, and I thought I would love to do it, it sounded like an amazing opportunity. I was nervous because I really wanted the job, so I turned up at The Church studio and met Siobhan and Marcy who were both so lovely and so welcoming, they diffused any anxiety. They had already recorded the album, so we were able to hear it properly when we were being auditioned to tour it, and they already had a guitarist, Gully, and they had a drummer, and together they made a fantastic rhythm section; so, I got in there and did my thing. And then I prayed! It was very quick, I heard back within a day or two that I had gotten the okay, so I had to tell the Wolfgangs and they were not pleased. But it was the right decision to do it.

Clare's time with Shakespears Sister proved fortuitous for several reasons, including the fact that it was while with them that she would meet one of the most important people in the development of her career, producer John Reynolds. Whilst rehearsing in [Fahey's husband] Dave Stewart's studio, The Church, in Crouch End, Reynolds showed up with bass player Matthew Seligman to work on demos with Nan Vernon, who was in The Spiritual Cowboys with Stewart. It was in this professional context that personal connections were forged, and the tightknit network was widened to include Clare. After that chance encounter a friendship ensued between her and Reynolds which would result in her inclusion on recordings and on the road with the likes of Sinead O'Connor, Indigo Girls, Damien Dempsey, and Brian Eno. Clare recalls,

> We all saw each other day-after-day when we would be outside taking a break. And I ended up going out with Matthew, so I was in a social scene which included John and he asked me to record a bassline for him. I was completely thrilled that he'd asked me, and it turned out to be for Sinead's song 'Thank You for Hearing Me' (1994). We recorded that in his studio in Durham Terrace and it came out extremely well; from then on, I've worked with him a lot. The way it seemed was that if John was the organizer/ MD behind the tour then he would bring in the musicians, and Sinead would like that as she'd have worked with us all before and there was a nice easy vibe but being in that high singer echelon, she had way too many other things to be concentrating on. The entire trust would be put into John's hands. If she went on tour with another MD, then it would be different musicians. I met the Indigo Girls when I was on the road with Sinead in the late '90s. We did the Lilith Fair tour a couple of times in a row and that was Sarah McLachlan's tour that she was told nobody would want to go see, it being bands with female lead singers, but she wiped the floor with Lollapalooza and all the rest of them for about three years solid. It was the most fantastic tour, with great food, great lighting and décor in the dressing rooms, proper mirrors etc., and in the tents where you'd gather to socialise it was lovely, they had these soft cushions, coffee machines, free bottled water, lights, scented candles, throws/blankets for if it got cold in the evenings. But then in the middle of the 1998 tour we went off to play the Fleadh for a weekend, which was just like loads of cans of warm beer in a bucket of water and a lot of mud. Some great bands but...! We couldn't wait to get back to the Lilith Fair tour. The Indigo Girls were on this tour as well and that year it was Sinead's band that drew every-one's interest because Sinead was on fire. The album was amazing, and the band was great, so lots of the other bands on the line-up would be on the side of the stage watching. Amy [Ray] and Emily [Saliers] hung out with us a lot; it was so much easier to blend in with the other artists on that tour. Usually, you are all in your sepa-rate 'tribes' and separate portakabins; everybody is a bit too shy to hang out and they don't want to intrude on other people's spaces. But we were in a great friendly mood, we always had a mirror ball and an amazing sound system with loads of reggae blasting out of

it, so we were basically inviting people to come and hang out with us, and the Indigo Girls were up for it. They hung out all the time and we became very good friends.

With such comradeship and connections made on the road, it would be only a matter of time before their friendship would turn into a professional association, thanks to the networking skills and musical nous of Reynolds, who would go on to produce the Indigo Girls' seventh studio album, *Come On Now Social*, in 1997. As a producer and as a musical director, Reynolds is a ringleader with a strong vision, and as such he hires strong players whom he knows will provide him with what he hears in his head. This means he doesn't change clientele very often, and so when an opportunity arises, there are a select few that he enlists; one of those first-call musicians is Clare, as she found out when the folk duo's bassist Sara Lee (she whose void in Gang of Four was filled by Gail Ann Dorsey, as noted in the previous chapter) left for pastures new. She says,

> I do think John always put together the dream team, and some-times these pesky bands come along but they already have a bass player, so I have to sit on the side-lines hoping that I can get at least one track. The Indigo Girls loved Sinead, loved our band, and loved John's production on her albums, so they basically poached us to join them on their new record. They decided they would record half the album in London with John and the other half of the album in Atlanta with Malcolm Burn. And they wanted me on both halves as the connection between the two. I did this amazing half of the record in London and then I went out to America to start work on the Atlanta part of the album. They had John play-ing drums in London and Brady Blade playing drums in Atlanta. Then after a couple of weeks, John was called over to Atlanta to take over production of that side of the record too – evidently his approach worked better for the girls. We toured and worked with them for years after that; we recorded an amazing album with them at Real World in 2019 which John Reynolds produced and played drums on. I was supposed to go on tour with them in 2020 but then Covid happened.

This was not the only tour on which Clare and Reynolds experienced the logistical difficulties of playing during a pandemic. In Christmas 2021, the bassist and drummer were in Dublin, Ireland to play a series of shows with local singer-songwriter Damien Dempsey, but what was supposed to be a tri-umphant four-night run in the capital's famous Vicar Street venue ended up reframed as six nights of early-evening shows at reduced capacity. Bemused by the situation that she and her bandmates found themselves in – namely,

of an unthinkable curfew in Irish nightlife – and worried about outright can-
cellations, Reynolds came to the rescue. Against management's inclination to
discard the Vicar Street residency altogether, Reynolds made sure the show
would go on, albeit reshuffling the show times and limiting capacity, remov-
ing standing room attendance, and adhering to the nationally mandated curfew of 8pm. Clare remembers,

> We were listening to all this business about a curfew in Ireland, and
> this was on the Friday night before we got our flight to Dublin. But
> John fought for it, and we got to play; he has been by Damo's side
> since Sinead first got him to listen to Damo's earliest cassettes. John
> got Damo immediately. John is such a fluent speaker of music. I've
> been in the room at times, and I have seen how he gets what an art-
> ist's unique thing is and how he can receive information and throw
> out ideas. He is so good at that kind of communication. We've
> worked together for so long that we've got so many unspoken touch
> points and reference points. It's about knowing that people get
> what you are going on about without having to labour over it. It's
> having to put your trust in somebody else that they'll understand
> enough that they'll give you the right thing. It makes the process so
> much easier when you've worked together for such a long time and
> you have those shared references, it makes everything go smoother.
> If John needs bass, then, fingers crossed, I'm in!

Thanks to Reynolds's recommendation, Clare found herself recording with
legendary soundscapist and former Roxy Music man, Brian Eno. Reynolds
and Eno were chatting during one of their regular walks through Hyde Park
when Eno mentioned that his bass player wasn't around and so he needed
someone to contribute some low end on a piece of music he was recording.
Despite maintaining a tight team of musicians that he always uses, Eno listened intently and acted upon it when Reynolds suggested, 'Why don't you
ask Clare?'

> I didn't know Brian at all, but he phoned me and then I went over to
> his studio. He is like a painter with music, he's got all these massive
> screens and has these soundscapes being built; he had a little bit of
> an idea that may have had some vocals on it, so I just spent a few
> hours there and I was allowed to dabble on this thing he was work-
> ing on, putting a bit of bass on it, some groove and some melody. It
> was lovely, and off I went! He uses all these other wonderful sounds
> and effects, so I couldn't quite identify what I played when the
> record came out [laughs]; it's not the typical verse-chorus-verse-
> chorus-middle-eight kind of music. And this was before I began
> choir singing with him. Brian has always been enthusiastic about

choral singing, community singing, and he's been doing it forever, since the '70s. He would participate in organizing choral singing in different venues, so he's got this group of people that come together occasionally, and we'll sing traditional songs, or maybe some old country numbers, or Everly Brothers songs. It's a very mixed bag and a lot of fun.

After putting in four decades providing solid sessions and live leg work for other people's music, Clare has found no immediate attraction to the kind of solo song writing or studio stability that many other touring players strive for after many years and much mileage clocked as dedicated road warriors. Rather, the bassist has recognized and come to accept that being a team player is what has sustained and satisfied her for such a long time. Happiness, it would seem for Clare, is in the act of collaboration.

I have been trying to put on my writing head, but I'm much better with other people than on my own. I have done some co-writing with Siobhan before on one of the Shakespears Sister albums, a lot of tracks on it are co-writes and we were very proud of those. But again, it was a team thing, and we have been planning to get together soon to play some guitar and see what happens. I do use Logic to do remote recording. It is great being able to record the bass from my little home (micro) studio because it means I have all the time in the world to think about what I want to play, or what else a track needs; I can do it again or edit it accordingly. In fact, when I was in France last year, I did a whole album for John remotely from there. I don't even know if the artist knew that this bass player who 'worked at the weekends' was really in France! I love being able to do that. And when I do eventually record something of my own it will probably be this wispy thing with a bit of a bass groove going on in the background. I don't think I can do 'songs' but I can certainly do a bass groove.

3 Susan Miller

On 18 November 1993, the Seattle band Nirvana recorded an acoustic set at the Sony Music Studios in Manhattan for what would be a live video and album release. That night, a simple wardrobe choice by singer Kurt Cobain would pique the curiosity of his fans who were rabid to consume anything he supported. He wore a Frightwig band t-shirt, and because of Cobain's choice of garb, the garment has, in and of itself, become an iconic symbol of the grunge movement and alternative music scene of the early 1990s. But for those who investigated the band beyond the branding, they would discover the seminal music of a group of young female punks who blazed a trail across America in the early 1980s and contributed to influencing generations of male and female rock artists for decades to come, whether they knew it or not. It is impossible to imagine the Riot Grrrl movement that sprang up in the 1990s happening without the artistic contribution of Susan Miller, Deanna Ashley, Mia Levin, and others who came and went throughout the line-up of Frightwig's early career. The band recorded their first album *Cat Farm Faboo* in 1984, and it was just prior to its release that Susan Miller joined the band as their second guitarist; she remained with the band for subsequent touring and for the recording of their 1986 follow-up album, *Faster, Frightwig, Kill! Kill!* Some of the other girl groups who emerged from the punk scene had smoothed out their sound and become more accessible for commercial consumption with each subsequent release. It seemed as though female representation within this musical milieu was being packaged and sold on a corporate level with little regard for the ethical values of the genre that characterized their inception. Evidently, ideology was not a big selling point once bands began making the charts. In truth, further female representation could be found, not on MTV or in the pages of *Rolling Stone*, but simmering in the underground movements wherein artists like Frightwig adhered to the aesthetic of the punk genre. They kept their strident expression of female empowerment and political ideals alive with no concessions made to corporatize their sound or dilute their rhetoric.

As such, there is a musical lineage in which the influence of the band can be traced to the emergence of the aggressively feminist resolve of the Riot Grrrl movement in the 1990s and in the hard-edged musicality of popular alt-rock acts like Hole and L7.

These days, Susan Miller leads a quieter life as a PhD holding professor at California's Palomar College, where she lectures in subjects such as Women's Studies and Social Psychology. Whilst preferring the hallowed halls of academia over the modest stages of punk-rock clubs, Susan distinctly recalls her days in the touring trenches, travelling the country in a caravan and meeting the future music stars long before the rest of the world knew their name.

> We must have gone back and forth across the country at least two or three times. That doesn't sound like a lot but for us it was insane in our little van. We were constantly going down to Atlanta or going up to Canada or Seattle. The famous image of Kurt Cobain wearing the Frightwig t-shirt on *MTV Unplugged* is because we played around Seattle so many times that he would come to our shows. I didn't know him; he was just another little fan, but Courtney used to hang out with us, she would follow us around. She was only a baby, she was so young back then, we would see her whenever we were going through the Northwest and Seattle, Oregon, Washington, and Canada. All those kids came to see us. They looked at each other and said, 'God, if these bitches can do it, so can we!'

Prior to spreading such influence with Frightwig, Susan had immersed herself in the musical underground of New York City, playing with avant-garde noise acts and radical punk bands that would contribute to her practical musical education. Planting herself in deepest, darkest East Village, the Californian born and raised Susan experienced a subculture vastly different to that which she was used to on the West Coast. 'The difference to me is night and day, and I think a lot of it is environment related', Susan considers.

> It's the difference between living on a razor's edge and living on a soft fluffy pillow. In New York, it doesn't matter who you are, you are going to work to survive. I used to get jobs playing The Pyramid Club, or Club 57 on St. Mark's Place, and some bars on Rivington Street. In San Francisco it is perpetually sunny, you can always be outside and that creates such a different vibe. You're not scratching and struggling to make enough money so that you are not outside on the streets, because there is a lot of community there. Whereas in New York it is edgy, the city is going to chew you up and spit you out unless you are very strong. But in San Francisco it's like 'let's get on SSI [Social Security] and let's party!' or they take over a squat.

It's just a different type of lifestyle. Being bi-coastal allowed me to see the real substantive difference in the two cultures. Back in the '70s and '80s you could come here with five-hundred bucks and find a place to live and get some shitty, crazy job or get on welfare or disability and live a pretty decent life. But New York back in our time was like *Taxi Driver*. When I moved there, I lived across the street from a Hell's Angels club. They ran the whole block. It was nuts! We hooked up with these people who sublet us an apartment and they tried to charge us $800 a month, which back then was a super amount of money for a little two-bedroom apartment on the Lower East Side. Then the landlord came to us and said, 'Hey, these people cannot sublet to you, the Hell's Angels put a gun to their head and told them to get off the block because they were dealing coke; so, if you want to live here the rent is $400 a month but those people are gone'. We were like, 'yeah!' The landlord told me right away we could live there but not to mess with the Hell's Angels; do not touch their bikes, do not make friends with them, just be cool. And we were.

Susan continues,

When Flipper would come to town on tour, they would park on the block, but their tyres would be slashed because the Hell's Angels would perceive them as a rival male gang; it was like, 'you can come visit these girls but don't park on our block'. Everyone sort of tip-toed around them, and I had every crazy person in New York come into my house, so I had to be careful. When Deanna showed up, I had to tell her not to go fucking one of these Hell's Angels, do not go to their clubhouse, and do not try to make friends with them. But of course, it's Deanna and she's like 'Hey, honey! Hey, baby! How ya doin'?' I was just thinking 'Don't do it!' They had their little ice cream carts from which they would sell their drugs. It was nuts, but I loved living there because I always felt safe. I never became friends with them, but I always felt that there was a bit of respect between us; they knew who we were, they knew I was playing in bands, and they would show up at gigs and stand in front of the door guarding it, they would help us move the equipment and even call us 'ma'am'; they were always on speed cleaning up the street! I swear, I got out of so much trouble by living on that block; the cops once tried to arrest me for graffiti, and I told them I live over on 3rd between 1st and 2nd and they were like 'oh...' and just backed off. The Hell's Angels ran that block, and they ran the police off that block, get back to your own fucking precincts!

Once firmly ensconced in NYC, Susan would gain experience in some unorthodox bands that would prepare her for the discipline of the hardcore bands to follow. For starters, she joined Spiritual Fire, an all-black experimental jazz outfit that would count the noted free jazz saxophonist Daniel Carter as part of the line-up. Carter would go on to appear on records by Yoko Ono, Yo La Tengo, and William Parker among many more, but before that he was also in another otherwise all-girl act with Susan called Psycho Sex which also featured Susan's West Coast pal Patti Ramelli as the lead singer, although 'singing' might be a mild euphemism for yelling and screaming about her Catholic guilt. The friends would collaborate in another band called Pure Schism, a defiantly avant-garde act that was comprised of no less than six bass players backed by Ramelli on drums. Susan recalls,

> We all played bass, so it was the heaviest heavy metal sound you could imagine, so heavy that we would empty a club! We had a Puerto Rican guy named Miguel who was our lead singer and he only had one word that he would say in every song and that was 'pain'. He would just scream the word 'pain' at the top of his lungs with all this heavy bass going on behind it and people would just clear out, nobody could take it; they would have to stand outside to listen because it was just too much. But to me that was a brilliant band, it was everything we wanted to say boiled down to its essence: one word, six basses, and drums … pain! It was the best band ever, but we only lasted three gigs.

Susan's instrumental experimentation extended to working with early drum machines and other electronic devices; she would explore the bowels of these machine like a mad scientist.

> Creating music with alternative approaches and experimentation was such a crucial part of my musical experience on 3rd Street. I had borrowed a Drumulator from my friend Amanda Kramer, who was living around the corner. This was the very first digital drum machine for consumers, built by Emu-Systems in conjunction with their revolutionary sampler The Emulator. This was a magical thing and of course all the punks would sneer and say, 'you can't replace a drummer!' But you could do a lot of creative things with it. I was not afraid to use anything, I would hook all these different devices together and try to find out what weird ass sounds we could make. And then when I got the Commodore 64 computer all bets were off! I learned how to program it because there were all these magazines that showed you how to program games, so that allowed me to mess with it and figure out a way to connect it to the music and trigger it so that everything would go haywire. I would

use it at these weird gigs that I was doing down at The Kitchen with Spiritual Fire. I would try to incorporate this Commodore 64 into the music, underlying the band's crazy improvisations with my flanger and distortion. It was as downtown as it gets. So much fun.

After much experimentation with various musical associates, Susan would get her first taste of the male-dominated hardcore punk scene when she joined her Bay Area pals Bad Posture as guitarist. The San Francisco band had relocated to New York City in 1982 to become part of the downtown underground scene that was the spawning ground for notable hardcore acts such as Sick of It All, Bad Brains, Cro Mags, and Agnostic Front. 'The Bad Posture guys followed me and Patti up to New York City', Susan says,

> My ex-husband Bruno was a founding member of the band with Emilio Crixell, Eddie Galvan, and John Surrel, but Bruno didn't follow them to New York, which meant they were missing a guitar player. At the time I was living in a sordid basement apartment and one day the lead singer of Bad Posture, 4-Way, calls me and says, 'I'm breaking up the band unless you join!' and I'm like, 'okay, this is not the perfect match here, you're playing speed psycho punk and I'm all over the place with this experimental stuff'. But 4-Way decided he had to have me in the band and I was sure the other guys were thinking, 'are you kidding me?' I used to sit for hours and hours with Emilio trying to learn these uber-fast Bad Posture songs and I had to fake it a little because they were technically difficult. I don't think people understand how hard it is to play that very fast style of music. It's muscular and precise, you can't be sloppy. As crazy as they were, the band was really on-point with their music.

And with that, Susan joined the band as they got in the van to tour all over the East Coast from the Jersey Shore up through Boston, Connecticut, New Haven, and up to Philadelphia, a route that they would repeat time and again. It was on these tours that Bad Posture would play alongside the likes of The Circle Jerks, G.B.H., Black Flag, and D.O.A., bands who were notorious for their raucous live shows, and through this Susan would get to experience first-hand the kind of aggression and disdain that could be levelled at female band members. 'It could be a shit-show!' Susan exclaims.

> I remember in the early years these little boys tended to love/hate me because I was generally the only woman in the situation onstage, it would be like, 'well, you play okay for a girl, I guess', and I would get beer cans thrown at me from the audience. It was wild, wild times. It was just massive chaos onstage because it was the height of the mosh pit, the circle pit, and crowd surfing. While I was

playing there would be people crashing and landing around me; it was so weirdly violent and yet somehow orchestrated, because there are rules. The most chaotic situation has its own rules and etiquette and mosh pits are like that; I had a real front row seat to it all because I was in the band. It was nuts. But we would be enticed to play by us being offered all the beer we could drink. 'Sign me up!'

After a year of craziness with Bad Posture and the New York downtown scene, the time came for Susan to move on when Frightwig rolled into town and invited her to join the band. The idea of enjoying some camaraderie with a group of women seemed far more appealing to the guitarist at that point. The band was already established in San Francisco and had just released *Cat Farm Faboo* on Subterranean Records, the independent label that was releasing important Bay Area punk records by Flipper and Dead Kennedys. Joining Frightwig was an opportunity for Susan to return to her West Coast musical roots and to the supportive community of clubs and artists that she had previously immersed herself in, where venues like The Club Foot would provide a stage for her bands such as The Wild Women and beatnik jazz outfit The Longshoremen. By 1986 Frightwig were poised to enter the studio to record their second LP, *Faster, Frightwig, Kill! Kill!* Released by Caroline Records, home to celebrated punk stalwarts Killing Joke, The Misfits, and Youth of Today, this brilliant sophomore album experimented with the band's hardcore sound by incorporating electronic and brass elements to create a typically discordant but often melodically-infused record that was unusually creatively progressive for the Californian punk scene of the mid-1980s. 'Caroline was supportive of us', Susan admits, 'but we signed a horrible deal with them which meant we made zero money in perpetuity. But they were decent to us, they took us on, as did Subterranean, the founder of which, Steve Tupper, was supportive of every band I was in'. Dodgy record deals aside, the album features songs like 'American Express' and 'I Don't Want to be Alone' which are an evolution of the genre and among the best of the band's catalogue; with this record Frightwig dared to take the punk aesthetic to sonic places that few other hardcore bands did. Susan admits,

> 'I Don't Want to be Alone' was one of my favourite songs in the studio. When we recorded that song, I was just like 'yes!' I was playing bass with a violin bow and doing all kinds of unusual stuff. There was a lot going on in the studio during the making of that record. We had Eric Drew Feldman from Captain Beefheart on keyboards, and he was amazing. But unfortunately, the engineers and the other people working at the studio weren't that open to letting a woman do anything … 'We'll handle it!' they'd say. You would tell them something doesn't sound right and that you want to do it such a way, but it would just lead to a lot of fighting. But

once we were in the recording studio it only took us about two-to-three weeks to finish the album. It was a lot of late nights because we couldn't really afford it, but we would get free studio time from 2am to 5am. So, while it didn't take very long to record that album, writing it took a little longer.

Susan continues,

I wrote 'American Express' when we were in Germany, I mean the song is literally our travelogue. We met this guy named Eddie and we cooked up this scheme for us to buy an American Express card and go to Hamburg to spend it all and then claim it was lost so we could try to scam everything. What a fucking mistake that was! I mean, German police, right? We declared the American Express cheques had gone missing and we wanted our money back, but they said they were going to investigate it and we ended up getting interviewed and drawn into it all. And of course, we were touring with D.O.A. and anti-American sentiment was running high because it was during the Reagan administration; people would say, 'take your fucking cruise missiles and shove them up your ass!' and 'you Americans are scum for the way you treat your black people!' It was just this intense hatred, and D.O.A. was from Canada so they weren't getting it at all, it was just us! So finally, we flipped out and said 'fuck you! We are American royalty; we are the granddaughters of Ronald Reagan and if you fuck with us, we will drop a fucking bomb right on your house!' We were telling all these punk rockers and these people in squats who hated us, 'look, bitch, you're smoking Marlboros, you're wearing Levis, you love Elvis Presley and James Dean, so don't talk to me about your hatred of America and how fucked we are as if we are political representations of their policies, because we hate them too!' But it just got out of control because I would have these long arguments in German bars with these boys who would tell me that the wall would never come down and that we turned away the Jews when they sent them to us in World War II, blah blah blah, all these crazy arguments. And that's how that song manifested.

With a new album to promote, Frightwig hit the road once again, but this would prove to be Susan's last ride with the band, culminating in a disastrous concert at the Sunset Strip venue, The Roxy Theatre, where they played with Scottish alt-rockers The Jesus and Mary Chain.

Everything dismantled for me that night at The Roxy. Deanna got into this huge fight with The Jesus and Mary Chain before the show, to the point where she dropped on her knees onstage and said 'fuck you, Jesus and Mary Chain! What do you want?! You want us to fucking pray to your fake-ass, pussy-boy bullshit?' And then during the show she broke a bass string and didn't have a replacement and wondered if they would give her one and I'm like, 'you are out of your fucking mind!' And then we ended up getting kicked out of our own show because they said we stole a bottle of vodka from their dressing room ... which we probably did. The promoter kicked us out and made us sit in the parking lot until the show was over. Sonic Youth was there as well, they were in the dressing room and calling for us to come in and party with them and we had to say, 'We can't! We're not allowed in'. That was the most punk thing we ever did, getting kicked out of our own show. But we probably did go into their dressing room and saw that they had all this shit while we didn't have anything, so we took a bottle of their vodka. We had to wait until the show was over before we could even get our equipment out. And that was the blow-out end of my musical career.

After the relative ignominy of being ejected from one's own show, the band returned to San Francisco, after which Susan had to confront some potentially life-changing issues that would have her reconsidering her life on the road. She had already come face-to-face with the harsh realities of touring whilst in Europe, tiring of the barrage of aggression at hardcore shows, and becoming increasingly aware of what the implications of maturing into her thirties meant for a female musician. Whilst on tour in Switzerland, Susan found herself staring out over Zurich in contemplation, whereupon she had an epiphany:

I thought, 'I'm thirty, I'm a woman, and I'm in this business? I might as well hang it up'. And especially in those days, if you're not cute and young and haven't made it by the time you are twenty-five then it's not going to happen for you. Then we had a crazy show there, which was just nuts, where someone tried to attack me on stage, and that just got me thinking, 'What the hell am I doing here? I have no money; I have no real career prospects... what the fuck!' So that sort of helped me move away from it. I felt like I did this thing and now I'm done with it. I was having that feeling of knowing that I had no education, no skills, and thinking, 'What can I do? What are my options? Go be a manager at a Taco Bell?' It wasn't like I could go and play in a lounge act. Then after The Roxy show in Hollywood we went back to San Francisco and that was where I went and got a pregnancy test. I didn't think I was pregnant, but I wanted to make sure. They told me it was negative, but I kept feeling like something was wrong and then I ended up getting another test and it was positive. I remember being really shocked and the world just kind of crashed down around me because I knew that if I am pregnant then I'm passed the point of being able to get an abortion or being able to do anything about it. So, I'm having this kid! I went to stay with Patti and being that she had a kid as well we just went into suburban serial mom mode in San Luis Obispo. Patti passed away in 2018, we had met when we were fifteen and were best friends for forty-five years. We were like twins, and we raised our kids together up to the age of four, which is when I was accepted into Berkeley. I went back to school and availed of every social service and welfare that you can imagine, food stamps and all of that, and slowly worked my way into this academic life. My major at Berkeley was Social Welfare and Public Policy, because I really understood social securities, food stamps, and all the planning that went into those programmes because I had been on all of them. I thought I wanted to be a social worker, but I found out quickly that I would be a terrible social worker. I did a lot of work in homeless shelters, at AIDS Crisis Drop-Ins and I knew I would last at it, so one of my mentors at Berkeley said I should get a PhD in Sociology and I was like 'okay!' And from there I got my doctorate and ended up going a different route altogether. I found out that I was better at school than I was at music.

Political and social causes have remained a constant in Susan's life, as crucial to her music as they are to her personal and scholastic endeavours. Her experiences in and observations of the social/cultural milieus of both the East and West Coast alternative musical movements are something that have informed her approach to her academic disciplines. They have instilled in her a lifelong empathy for the kinds of sociological issues that the best punk music can shine a light on. She says,

I saw how bad and out of control the Bay Area was even before I got into the music scene there. I had lived on Castro Street and South of Market and my communities were literally destroyed. Whether it was my friends, the people I hung out with, or the people I got up to bad behaviour with, you name it, I was convinced that we were all going to die at some point. I remember meeting Richard Hell and he had some interesting observations. I first met him when he was on tour in San Francisco in September of 1983. We were introduced at my friend's loft in South of Market. Jim Storm's place. I showed him some lyrics of a song I was working on, and he said, 'do you wanna jam?' We went back to my place on 3rd and Bryant and played for hours because we were on speed. When I moved to NYC in 1984, I met up with him again, and by then AIDS/HIV was everywhere. One day Richard said, 'you know, I think it's like a conspiracy to kill off gay people and Black people'. That was the first time I ever heard somebody articulate that, which is not that crazy.

Over the ensuing decades, Susan remained committed to raising awareness of social ills and encouraging intellectual discourse on such, leading to her present position in which she is doing so from the more controlled confines of the classroom than from the chaotic stages of punk clubs. Remaining true to her lifelong adherence to the punk movement's ethical principles, Susan's academic work, as it was with her musical output, is informed with a politically charged and socially compassionate resolve achieved with a sympathetic eye and advocacy for human frailty, feminist causes, and cultural injustice.
Susan affirms,

All of the Frightwig songs were very subversive, the music that I wrote and co-wrote always had a total 'fuck the world!' vibe to it. Our sentiments were, 'this is so unfair!' and ''there's so much inequality!' and 'quit fucking with women!' although we did it our own way, we weren't shouting, 'I'm a feminist!' In my graduate education I ended up really getting into Mathematics and Statistics, so my expertise is in quantitative methods and research methods, which is all within Sociology. I did my dissertation looking at women whose partners were incarcerated at San Quentin prison, really examining those relationships. The question was why would a woman stay with a man who is in fucking prison? What is the connection there? They are extremely committed to these relationships and that's what I was looking at. I spent a year going to San Quentin for this research. After a while you are like a fly on the wall and people really start talking to each other as if you don't exist. This population was very Oakland, that is to say Black and poor; it's not a middle-class demographic that is in mass incarceration. It was such a shift in perspective for me because they would talk about things that weren't part of my reality. Education does that. And I would say that having a musical education and experience really expands how you think and helps you realise how much of a universe is out there beyond our own immediate world.

4 Tracy Wormworth

The name Wormworth is a recognizable one to those with an interest in American music culture. If it rings familiar it is because several generations of one particular Wormworth clan have left an indelible imprint across some major musical movements and genres. Emerging out of Utica, New York in the late 1950s as a drummer of note, Jimmy Wormworth II is synonymous with the world of jazz and blues, having accrued over the last seven decades a considerable discography of recordings with innovative and ground-breaking jazz artists such as Annie Ross, Jon Hendricks, Lou Donaldson, Charlie Rouse, and Julius Watkins. His son James Wormworth was a television regular as a member of the house band on *The Tonight Show with Conan O'Brian*. Soaking up the influence of her brother and father was Tracy Wormworth, current bass player for The B-52s and erstwhile side musician with the likes of Sting, Cyndi Lauper, Wayne Shorter, and a host of talent from across the musical spectrum.

Tracy grew up in Bed-Stuy, Brooklyn, before it became fashionably gentrified, with her parents and four siblings. When she was twelve years old, her parents separated, and as a result her time would be split between New York City and upstate New York. Her mother moved to the former industrial belt city of Utica, where Tracy would spend her early teen years. 'We would go back and forth', she says, 'we moved with my mother to upstate New York, and we were there for five years and then when I was about sixteen or seventeen I came back down to New York to stay with my father. I stayed in the city from then on. I spent the first three years of high school in Utica, and I finished down here in New York, which was goofy'.

Growing up in New York of the 1960s and 1970s meant Tracy could be bombarded with all manner of cultural explosions, from the jazz subculture that was her father's domain to the emerging countercultural sounds that were permeating the market and overtaking the radio waves. Tracy would be exposed to her parents' Motown records and the soulful funk rock of Sly and the Family Stone who were introducing a new kind of groovy, cross-cultural, genre-bending sound. The music played and enjoyed by her father and brother would instil in her a fascination with jazz, particularly the burgeoning fusion genre, with its intoxicating blend of unconventional, improvisatory elements that married jazz, rock, and rhythm and blues.

My brother James was playing music before I ever picked up a bass, he started playing as a younger child. He had established a professional career relatively early; before I started playing. His musical taste and influences had a profound impact on me because he kind of taught me what to listen to and who to listen to. I ended up loving the music that he loved. The precursor to that was my mother and father, who listened to Motown. I grew up in the 60s and 70s, so I was listening to Sly and the Family Stone and all that stuff. My father listened to all kinds of jazz, and he also listened to classical music. We listened to a little bit of everything, we even listened to sound recordings from car races, which was kind of interesting. But we listened to a lot of different things in our house. There was this radio station called WRVR and it used to play Jaco Pastorious, Lenny White, and stuff like that. My brother really got into the fusion thing and that's really what we listened to during those formative musical years. I loved Jaco and I really love Anthony Jackson. I used to go see Anthony play live and he used to play this six-string bass that I used to call 'The Christmas Tree Bass' because it had red and green lights all over it. But the thing about Anthony is the way that he plays, especially when I used to see him live. I could sit there and close my eyes and I could see the notes taking up the whole space of the beat, it was like a big giant ink dot. Just listening to him was amazing, as seeing him playing live. He is definitely one of my bass heroes, as is Marcus Miller. Other heroes of mine are Paul Chambers, an upright player who performed with Miles [Davis] for years, and Ron Carter (another collaborator of Davis whose work also includes credits with Roberta Flack, Billy Joel, and Duke Pearson). I'm kind of enamoured with the bass players of yesteryear. When I started playing, we had a family band – not with my father, but just my sister, my brother, and I. My mother and younger brother were not musicians, although he became a roadie a little later, but that was the closest he got to it. Some family friends who were musicians joined our band as well. My first gig was in that group, so to speak, and that's because the mother of one of my friends in the band got us our first gig at a dinner party or something like that. So that was where I started playing live. I would see a lot of live music because I used to go to my father's gigs quite often, and that was because he always wanted someone to take down his drum set or whatever. I was like an indentured servant!

Tracy's interest in playing music arose in earnest as she was dating a particularly well-known bass player, the aforementioned Marcus Miller. He was a celebrated session musician who had played on the likes of Miles Davis's *The Man With the Horn* (1981) and *Star People* (1983), Aretha Franklin's *Get It Right* (1983), and Luther Vandross's *Never Too Much* (1981), amongst many other notable recordings. However, it was his evident ease with the bass guitar that had Tracy interested in the instrument as much as with him. According to her,

> I started playing because of Marcus. He was very busy here in New York on the studio scene at the time and now he's a really accomplished player, composer, arranger, and songwriter. Back then I would go to his gigs all the time and I used to sit there and say, 'oh, I can do that!' Which was really naïve and silly, and wishful on my part; it was childlike thinking, but I thought maybe I could do it in some capacity. So, he gave me a bass, and then after he gave me the bass we split up. We were young, we were teenagers, almost adults. He told me, 'Don't let it collect dust', and I became so attached to it and enamoured by it that I was just stuck to it. I would take it to my job when I was doing temp work. I would practise on it at lunchtime. I would sleep with it in bed and take it into the bathroom... it came with me everywhere! I took it very seriously. I started studying and taking lessons in how to read. I was basically trying to emulate Marcus.

A chance encounter with a stranger on the streets of New York City in 1982 led to Tracy being given an opportunity to parlay that intense love of her bass into a professional association with The Waitresses, a promising new wave band out of Akron, Ohio who were seeking a new bass player whilst recording their debut album *Wasn't Tomorrow Wonderful?*

> I was working a 9 to 5 job, where I used to take my bass with me, and so I left one day and this guy stopped me in the street and said, 'hey, is that a bass?' and I said, 'yeah...' and he said, 'I know a band that's looking for a bass player. Are you interested?' And I'm like, 'I'll play with anybody! Yes, please!' I was just so eager to play. So, he gave me Chris Butler's number and he gave Chris my information, so I called him, and he was like, 'okay, can you come and rehearse?' or audition, basically. And I had to go to his apartment. Nowadays you would probably think twice about doing that, but back then you would just do it. I got there and he said, 'let's play a blues', and we did, and he was like, 'you're hired!' The blues! That's what I was doing: jazzy, bluesy fusion. I played everything. And that was a goal of mine, I wanted to be able to play everything.

The Waitresses were founded by Butler and included former Television drummer Billa Ficca, future Psychedelic Furs saxophonist Mars Williams, and were fronted by Patty Donohue whose distinctive deadpan vocal delivery offered up healthy doses of irony with her melody. After Tracy replaced original bass player Dave Hofstra, this line-up would release two albums, 1982's *Wasn't Tomorrow Wonderful* and the following year's *Bruiseology*, and the EP, *I Could Rule the World If I Could Only Get the Parts*, which would yield a perennial holiday hit in the form of 'Christmas Wrapping'. 'In the beginning, The Waitresses was a shoestring budget kind of thing', Tracy admits, 'so we were riding around in vans with the equipment in the back and taking turns sleeping on the equipment. It was what it was. But when I listened to those records decades later, I thought, "we were kicking ass!" and then the band broke up sometime in 1983'.

After The Waitresses Tracy would hone her studio and live skills further when her friend, jazz guitarist Rodney Jones, brought her into the world of recording music for television shows. Two hit sitcoms that Tracy would contribute to the soundtracks for were NBC's *The Cosby Show* and its subsequent spinoff *A Different World*. Jones would be responsible for bringing Tracy in on a variety of projects, including an album for iconic Old Hollywood songstress Lena Horne, *We'll be Together Again* (1994) and a recurring stint on live television. Tracy says,

> Rodney could be my guardian angel sometimes, musically-speaking, he kind of took me under his wing for some reason – I guess he liked my playing – and he brought me into the session thing doing the background music for television. I did all the seasons of *The Cosby Show* and *A Different World* in the early '80s; I did it for the whole time that they ran. Because Rodney brought me into that, it springboarded me into other things. He got me into the Lena Horne album, and I was definitely a fish out of water with that.

Another job that Jones helped book for Tracy was as the bass player for *The Rosie O'Donnell Show* house band. Such a gig allowed Tracy some steady employment across several years of it being broadcast, as well as the opportunity to provide the music for many acts of varied musical styles. Much of the guest material would require a versatile musician capable of playing the double bass when a song required it. However, this was an instrument that Tracy had no experience with, but so eager for the job was she that this minor drawback would not impede on her ability to at least wing it through some showtunes. Working for a Broadway buff such as Rosie O'Donnell meant that many big band arrangements would have to be performed by her house band. 'I was desperate', she admits.

I was having one of those years where I wasn't working much at all and when Rodney called me from the audition I heard this music in the background, and I said, 'where are you?' and he replied, 'oh, I'm at an audition for this TV show'. So, I asked him, 'do they need a bass player?' He said 'they do, but they need somebody who plays upright bass', and I said, 'tell them I play upright! I need a job!' I didn't play double bass at all. I faked my way through playing the upright bass with Liza Minnelli! Thank God the song was in the key of A, which meant it was all open strings. I drew chalk lines on the fretboard so I could see where I was going; it was so sad. Rosie is a huge Broadway aficionado, and she had done Broadway too. Our MD on the show, John, was also from that world and so there was a lot of Broadway on the show. We did a lot of that stuff, and especially so during Tony season. The show would be broadcast live from 10am to 11am and you had to be there from 7.30 in the morning, but when anything from Broadway came on the show, we had to be there for 5am. We used to play with Barry Manilow and Bette Midler a lot because they would come on all the time and then we ended up doing a live *Today Show* thing with them. We also did a lot of those Comedy Central Roast shows too. That was a very cool situation. And it taught me how to be on time! If live TV taught me anything, it taught me punctuality. But it is all because of Rodney that I got into that television world, he is responsible for getting me the jobs on *The Cosby Show*, *A Different World*, and the *Rosie O'Donnell Show*.

Whilst Tracy was continuing her session work on TV hit sitcoms, she also began playing with singer-songwriter and award-winning Broadway actress, Phyllis Hyman, and she remained with her for several years until 1987, when the biggest gig of her career would take her on the road for two years straight. Tracy was dating a member of Sting's touring band on the *Dream of the Blue Turtles* tour, which allowed for the occasional trip to the Caribbean to catch up with her boyfriend as well as with some sunshine. Following the exhaustive two-year tour for that album, Sting and his musicians would set up camp in Monserrat to record *Nothing Like the Sun* at Air Studios.

When they were recording *Nothing Like the Sun* in Monserrat I went down there because I'm like, 'yeah, I'm coming to that! I'm getting away from this frickin' winter'. I would go to the studio and hangout. Then fast-forward to when they were putting together the *Nothing Like the Sun* tour; Sting invited me to audition to be the bass player. He knew that I played bass because he would talk to me about it, but I don't think he had ever heard me play. He was just going on the word of the guys in the band who knew me. I had played with Mino Cinélu, who was Sting's percussionist, so Mino said that it was him that got me the gig, lol!

Nothing Like the Sun, which produced the hit single 'Englishman in New York', elevated Sting's status as a solo artist as the ensuing tour for the album would take him and his band to some of the world's biggest stages through-out 1987 and 1988. For this high-profile global trek, Sting surrounded him-self with some of the most eminent musicians available, including Branford Marsalis on saxophone, Jeffrey Lee Campbell on guitar, Kenny Kirkland and Delmar Brown on keyboards, percussionist Mino Cinélu, Jeal-Paul Ceccarelli (followed by J.T. Lewis) on drums, and Tracy Wormworth on bass. Having gone from playing modest clubs with The Waitresses and Phyllis Hyman to now playing five nights at Wembley Arena as well as colossal football stadi-ums in South America, and everywhere else in-between, Tracy found herself experiencing a whole new realm of live performance which tested her nerves. She was now being exposed to millions of people, laying down the groove alongside one of the biggest pop stars on the planet. 'That tour, playing those massive stadiums, was so overwhelming', she reveals,

> we started rehearsing in '87 and then we did a world tour through-out all of '88. I was definitely wet behind the ears! I was used to playing gigs in clubs in New York and wedding band dates. On the outside I was like [calm expression] 'okay, we're just going to go out and play', but on the inside I was like 'ahhhh!' I was freak-ing losing it! The first live show that we played on that tour was in Brazil, at Rio de Janeiro's *Estádio do Maracanã*, which was this 200,000-seater stadium, and before that we played *Saturday Night Live*. So, I was petrified, but...

And while playing with the pre-eminent pop stars of the day casts more eyes upon you, it also gave some of those in the position of power of hiring musicians a false indication that Tracy was out of their price range, as she explains: 'what happens after you do a tour like that is that people think, "okay, we can't hire her, she's too expensive", and that meant that I had lean times after that tour, because people wouldn't hire me'. But Tracy didn't have to wait around too long before going back out on the road, although this time the venues were not sports arenas and stadiums, but jazz clubs and theatres. Then she started playing with saxophonist Wayne Shorter. In 1990, Tracy joined forces with keyboardist Jim Beard, drummer Terri Lyne Carrington, and percussionist Lenny Castro in forming a considerable quartet of musi-cians to ably support the former Miles Davis sideman and Weather Report founder on his travels across Europe and Japan. 'I went on the road with Wayne again in 1995', Tracy recalls, 'Wayne has a penchant for female musi-cians and one of his favourite people on the planet is Terri Lyne Carrington, who is an incredible drummer and songwriter and activist, and I think it might have been her who recommended me, but I don't know'.

Taking her back to bigger stages, Tracy would go on to work with a variety of major artists throughout the 1990s, including Cyndi Lauper, Sophie B. Hawkins, and Joan Osbourne, although it would be a connection from the jazz fusion world which led to her work with pop stars Paula Abdul and Des'ree, as she recalls:

> I used to play with a drummer named Rocky Bryant, who was from a band called The Family Stand. I used to love playing with him, we were with Mino Cinélu, and later Geri Allen, and we would do other things around New York together. Rocky then got me into recording some things with two of the guys who were the leaders of The Family Stand, particularly their founder Peter Lord Moreland, who was producing Paula Abdul and Des'ree. Peter went on to start his own band in the early '90s called Icon Gypsy, but it never took off unfortunately; it was great music, but I guess it just wasn't the right timing. With Cyndi Lauper I did this weird promo tour thing which was just in Europe. It was for some reggae project she was doing, like remixes of her previous songs done in a reggae style, and we did a lot of TV, especially in London. It was an all-female band, it was fun. I did a lot of promo tours with people, including Sophie B. Hawkins and Joan Osbourne; I did a lot with Joan and the first came about when 'One of Us' came out and again when the *Righteous Love* album came out. I really loved the tour that I did with Joan when we were opening for The Dixie Chicks. We were playing arenas and I loved the way their whole operation ran, they really had it together, and we were opening so we were only playing for thirty minutes in front of 15,000 people, so I was like, 'Yo! This is awesome!' And that tour sold out in like two minutes. They were huge. The only downside was it was the period where the Chicks said 'F-George Bush' so there was some controversy and a lot of stress-related stuff going on. They were getting a lot of threats so they would have to sweep the arenas. That was kind of a drag.

While Tracy has put her stamp on plenty of albums and tours within the pop and jazz realms, that didn't stop her from getting the call to audition for some of the world's biggest hard rock acts. Tracy had brief dalliances in the company of former Van Halen frontman David Lee Roth and former Generation X vocalist Billy Idol at the height of their respective solo stardom and MTV exposure. 'The David Lee Roth situation was interesting', Tracy reveals.

Marcus [Miller] had this business manager, someone who kind of organised his scheduling, and he was supposed to do that session but couldn't make it. And I was talking to this manager at the time wondering if I could use her services, and it was she who referred me for that session. So, I got there, and it was all the top A-list musicians, and I was just like…! And this was for a demo that he was spending a fortune on; we did about three or four songs, but it was for a record that never came out. And with Billy Idol I walked in there and was like, 'are you sure you guys wanted me to audition?!' I walked in and everybody was covered in safety pins from head to toe. I could probably have fit in at some point, but I wasn't going to be as hardcore as they were. I have no idea how I ended up being recommended for that one. I just thought, 'I don't fit into this', but maybe I ended up on their radar because of The Waitresses.

Tracy wouldn't have been the only Waitress to join Idol for his popular brand of power pop, as her former colleague Mars Williams provided saxophone for the peroxide punk on occasion in the 1980s.

While most musicians will have some 'what could have been' moments where coveted jobs ultimately proved tantalizingly elusive, no doubt the biggest gig that got away from Tracy was The Rolling Stones. The legendary British band had just wrapped up their Steel Wheels/Urban Jungle Tour in 1991 when original bass player Bill Wyman left the group for good. After taking a break in 1992, during which each Stone released solo projects, the band reconvened the following year to record their 20th studio album, *Voodoo Lounge*. But now the band were bass-less and thus began auditioning for Wyman's replacement. On the recommendation of G.E. Smith, the guitar player for the *Saturday Night Live* house band and who had played on Mick Jagger's solo releases, the singer would make a phone call to Tracy, which led to her having a memorably surreal afternoon playing the blues with The Rolling Stones.

'Mick Jagger actually called me!' Tracy enthuses.

I was working on a musical project for a friend of mine, James McBride, who is a world-renowned writer. We were workshopping the musical, and I was staying in a hotel and the front desk called me and said, 'there's a call for you here at the front desk', and I was like, 'really?!' So, I picked it up and Mick Jagger's assistant said, 'is this Tracy? Mick Jagger would like to speak with you'. And I'm like, 'yeah. Sure'. I thought somebody was playing a joke on me but then he got on the phone, and I was like, 'oh, shoot! Okay, this is not a joke!' I played Sadowsky basses, and I thought it was Roger Sadowsky that referred me, but Mick told me G.E. Smith had referred me. But the thing is I had never met him! But you just never know who takes notice of you and can recommend you. I don't really know how it happens, it's kind of word of mouth here in New York, someone says, 'you need a bass player? I know a bass player…' that's kind of the way it goes. That audition and the one for Billy Idol are the two auditions where I was thinking, 'what am I doing here?' And one of these things is definitely not like the other. They told me what songs to learn, and I went to the audition wearing a Thelonious Monk t-shirt because I knew that Charlie Watts was a big jazz fan, and I love Thelonious Monk. And he really liked that.

Unfortunately for Tracy, another bass player was auditioning and his bona fides within the jazz world were cemented with his work on the Miles Davis albums *Decoy* (1984) and *You're Under Arrest* (1985). Darryl Jones, whom Tracy had previously replaced as Sting's touring bass player, had accrued some notable credits throughout the 1980s with his recorded contributions to successful albums for Patti LaBelle (*Patti*, 1985), Philip Bailey (*Inside Out*, 1986), and Eric Clapton (*Journeyman*, 1989). Considerable credits to be sure, but it was his association with Miles Davis that piqued Rolling Stones drummer Charlie Watts's interest and was sure to edge out any other competition. 'Charlie already had his heart set on Darryl', Tracy reveals.

Charlie really wanted him because he had played with Miles and ultimately Charlie made the decision to hire Darryl based on that experience, and I respect that. Word came back to me that the gig could have been mine, so I missed that gig by that much. And Darryl is an incredible bass player, so I understand why Charlie made that decision because he was the drummer. I'm just thankful that I got to be in that room for a hot second. It was an amazing experience. And of course, I had to play the blues again. It's always about the blues.

While many artists have come and gone during the navigation of Tracy's lauded career trajectory, one act has taken precedence more than any other. At this stage, as much a family as they are musical colleagues and comrades, The B-52s has been a perennial part of Tracy's life on-and-off (though mostly on) for over three decades now. When incumbent bass player Sara Lee took a hiatus from the Athens, Georgia, band in the early 1990s to go and work with the Indigo Girls, this meant that there were some serious shoes to fill. However, Alyson Palmer, the singer and bassist of the cabaret-rock band BETTY, knew exactly who would fit the sartorial as well as musical profile required. Palmer was a mutual friend of Tracy and B-52s singer Kate Pierson and she duly recommended that Tracy be the one to step into the considerable void left by Lee. And she did, becoming a permanent live fixture in the band as well as recording bass on various tracks for the albums *Good Stuff* (1992) and *Funplex* (2008). For Tracy, becoming a B would be an opportunity to experience the wild world of kitsch new wave that yielded such unique early albums as *Wild Planet* (1980), *Bouncing off the Satellites* (1986), and their commercial breakthrough, *Cosmic Thing* (1989). 'They are such a fun band!' Tracy exclaims.

> I love playing their earlier stuff because it is so quirky and because their punkier stuff is kind of raw – it's the kind of stuff that makes you go, 'what the hell were they thinking?' Right now, we're try-ing to present the best show that we can and hopefully it comes across. A few years ago, we did some shows with an orchestra at The Hollywood Bowl, and I wish we would do more of those kinds of engagements because that was killer! We performed with orchestras all around the country. We played with the Boston Pops, we played with the LA Philharmonic, and with the National Symphony. It was awesome. I loved that!

As it has with many of those profiled within these pages, New York City has shaped Tracy's musical, as well as personal, identity. It was the town that enabled her to carve out a credible career as the various vibrant music scenes afforded Tracy many stages to showcase her considerable chops and dazzling stage presence. Across the city's venues, be they modest or massive, the right people looked on and took note of this mercurial musical maven. Whether it was for improvisational jazz, rough and ready rock, or polished pop, Tracy Wormworth had you covered.

> I don't live in New York anymore and I do miss it for sure, as that is where my musical life is for the most part. But I'm so far from any musical projects right now. When you are not in New York you are kind of out of sight and out of mind. I'm lucky that I'm playing with The B-52s because everybody in that band has their own lives. So, we all come together to play and tour and everything else when we need to, but we also stay in touch with each other when we're not together. They're kind of like my other family to some degree because I've been with them for so long off and on. We got each other through the pandemic for sure, even though we weren't working. We even have a band thread which is full of Fred [Schneider]'s jokes and amusing commentary. They are such a cool, awesome band and I love them all.

5 Joy Askew

Many of the musicians interviewed in this book found their tribe in the down-town music scene of New York City. Some of them are indigenous tri-staters, while others came from afar to immerse themselves within the artistic circles that thrived there in the 1970s and 1980s. Joy Askew is one of those who trav-elled across the Atlantic to establish a new musical life for herself in NYC, having grown up in the North of England of the 1950s and 1960s. Joy's was a musical household wherein some of her earliest memories are of singing along to her parents' radiogram trying to imitate Ella Fitzgerald. It was through the warm, fuzzy speakers of that oversized piece of furniture that she enjoyed the sounds of Louis Armstrong and Nellie Lutcher. It wasn't just a home of music appreciation, but one of performance, as her father also played clarinet, double bass, and piano; he could reproduce Bach's 48 Preludes and Fugues or Teddy Wilson's jazz standards with ease. So, it is no surprise that music would shape and define the life of Joy Askew. Joy says,

> My father was a really great musician, although he wasn't a pro-fessional one. He was an educator in Newcastle, and he was in local orchestras as well, so he was well-known among many in Newcastle; you just had to say his surname and they knew who he was. The double bass was always in the house, and I can remember being very small, about five or six, and standing on a stool trying to play it. It hurt the hands, but I was fascinated by it. We had to go up to bed early, by about seven o'clock, and that's when dad would start to play piano and he usually played in the dark, he didn't need to turn the light on; we used to call out requests, but we had no idea what the names of the tunes were, so we would sing them, 'Play the one that goes [*sings melody*]…!' and then he would start playing that one. They were all jazz standards. I realized years later that was

my setting for both jazz and classical music. My mum and dad used to sing *Porgy and Bess*, so I got to know a little bit of that as well.

In 2017, Joy released an album entitled *Queen Victoria*, the brass sounds of which evokes the musical atmosphere of her Newcastle adolescence. With nostalgia in its grooves, Joy's compositions are rounded out by the Brighouse and Rastick Brass Band, the long-established West Yorkshire ensemble which Joy brought on to the record to recall a fog-shrouded northern landscape throughout which blew an omnipresent musical wind:

> Brass was prevalent when I was growing up, to the point where you didn't notice it. We were interested in The Rolling Stones and The Beatles, meanwhile there's the sound of this brass blowing all around us and in the background. You didn't think it was worth anything because it was going on all the time and we had something new which was exciting and which interested us, but about ten years ago I had a sudden memory of being out on my street and leaning against the garden wall; it was very foggy, as it is in Newcastle, and in the distance I heard a sound. It may have been the Salvation Army practising, but no matter who it was, the sound of a brass band is unmatchable, it's a definite sound. And I was hearing this music coming from half-a-mile away, then a quarter-of-a-mile away, getting closer, but I could never see them, only hear them. The thing that fascinated me about it was the atmosphere that this incredible sound was creating; it was the fog, the mist, the dirt, the filth in the air, and God knows what else. It sounded like it felt, and it felt like it sounded. By the time I was making *Queen Victoria* I was much older and more mature, I was interested in what it was and how this memory just made me go 'wow!' It was amazing. So, I started listening to recordings by the Grimethorpe Colliery Band and I thought how interesting it would be to write the songs that I write here in Brooklyn, New York City and just smash them together with that sound.

While brass was part of the fabric of Northern music culture, the imported sounds of the blues were informing the emerging counterculture of British youth and began to make their way up North at just the right time – from the Delta to Doncaster, so to speak – thanks to the likes of Eric Burdon and Georgie Fame. Of course, this American aesthetic was also crucial to the sound and song writing of the biggest acts to come out of England in this period: The Beatles, The Rolling Stones, Fleetwood Mac, Cream, The Yardbirds, Ten Years After, and many more whose licks and shuffles scored the revelry of many mod clubs throughout the land, creating a new musical movement that was also known as the British Blues Boom and influencing a generation of musicians in the process. 'That's what I was getting into', Joy affirms.

> I was thirteen by the time the blues boom had hit in England and fortunately I had an older brother, Roger, who loved this. He had this big clunky acoustic guitar and then got an electric guitar for his birthday. He would keep me in the bedroom with the acoustic guitar where he would make me play this basic blues rhythm pattern repeatedly while he practised his blues soloing over and over in the key of E!

For sure, this movement (and particularly bluesman John Mayall) gave birth to the first generation of UK guitar heroes, such as Mick Taylor, Peter Green, Keith Richards, and Eric Clapton, all of whom contributed to creating a new wave of pop-culture iconography in England. 'It was pop-culture, it really was!' Joy concurs.

> The blues thing in England was explorative. You can hear Clapton pushing ahead and into where he was going to go. And when Cream came out, I joined the Cream fan club. I played with Jack [Bruce, from Cream] in 1988 and I didn't want to tell him I had been in the Cream fan club. I played a show in Madison Square Garden with him. I'd been in the fan club many years earlier and there I was standing in a dressing room before going out on stage to play, talking to him, and he's asking me 'What album is this track (of Cream's) on?' and I know the answer, but he doesn't! Jack was a genius, and I knew that when I was fourteen, and just to get that opportunity to stand next to him on stage was incredible. As well as the blues you had all the colour of The Beatles; we got 'Twist and Shout' and then it developed, so by the time we got 'Tomorrow Never Knows' you are right with it, you are growing up with it. I realize now that I grew up with their speedy development of exploration and I also think that shaped me because I am never looking to copy myself, thanks to experiencing these guys who were creating and discovering like crazy.

She continues,

> I was a huge fan of the first Fleetwood Mac album, the one with the trash can on the cover. I got to see them play in a tiny club in Ashington and ended up talking to them all. I loved Chicken Shack with Christine Perfect on keys, who became Christine McVie. I adored her. I got to see John Mayall, I got to see Mick Taylor. It was an amazing time. And when you think of the North of England you

think of Eric Burdon. There's a clear division between the people who can sing the blues and who can't, but Eric Burdon could sing the blues, you can hear it when you listen to 'The House of the Rising Sun'.

Joy's first taste of professional music life occurred when she was eighteen years old and whilst enrolled in her second term in the art school at Newcastle University. The college held all-nighter socials which attracted acts to perform for the imbibing student body, and one particular evening they were due to host singer Paul Jones, who was being backed by Pete Brown & Piblokto! Brown had an association with Joy's favourites, Cream, having co-written several of the band's songs with Jack Bruce and Eric Clapton, but for this show he was providing backing for Jones, who by this point had broken away from Manfred Mann and had starred in Peter Watkins's 1967 film, *Privilege*. Unfortunately, the van carrying Brown and his band broke down on the way to the venue, leaving Jones without musicians. Enter Joy and Roger Askew. Joy recalls,

> Paul Jones had arrived from London but Pete Brown and his Piblokto were stuck in Doncaster, so they never made it. At this stage I already had about four years of experience of performing with local Newcastle bands with my brother, and we were there at this college all-nighter along with our drummer and bass player, so when word got out that Pete Brown and his band couldn't make it, the organizers began rushing through the audience looking for us; they had seen us come in and knew we could play. So, they found us and were like, 'Joy! Roger! Can you get up and back Paul Jones?' It was a full house, and he had no band! What are we going to say, 'No!'? So, we said we would do it and they took us into the dressing room and Paul is there looking at us, I mean we must have looked like ruffian kids, wide-eyed and ridiculous. So, he said, 'Why don't you go on and play first and then I'll come out and play'.

Knowing there was a grand piano onstage, Joy and her comrades decided to play the obscure Aynsley Dunbar Retaliation song, 'Cobwebs', on which they would be joined by Jones playing harmonica. They filled the rest of the time playing blues shuffles, the experience of which clearly impressed the pop star, as Joy recalls:

> Paul took my phone number and called the next day saying, 'I want you to come down to London and join my band'. I only went to Art College for the first year when Paul asked me to go to London. I went, but I didn't stay. We were back and forth. We played some shows; we played at The Marquee, and we played the Empire Pool

which was Wembley, and he had me sing 'Cobwebs'. Another song
we did was Sam and Dave's 'Thank You' and we sang it in thirds all
the way through. Paul's voice was so spectacular, the guy is really
a great blues singer.

It would be another year before Joy would fully embrace a move to London
and engage in its vibrant rock music milieu, joining an all-girl group called
Bitch. It was whilst living in the capital that she became fascinated with jazz
music, thanks to the lead guitarist of Bitch, Inger Jonsson-Smith, whose
husband Terry Smith happened to be the guitarist with the noted jazz-rock
fusion band, If, and who had been named 'Best Jazz Guitar Player in the
World' in a *DownBeat* magazine poll. Hanging out with Smith, Joy was introduced to milestone jazz albums by Cannonball Adderley, Miles Davis and
John Coltrane, engendering a love of the genre that would consume her to
this day. Their friendship would also provide Joy with the kind of education
that a music school could never do, the personal curation of an artform by a
practitioner willing to share their passion and insights with a voracious listener. Joy recalls,

> Terry had a fantastic record collection, and he would sing, he
> said you have to learn to sing everything, and he would sing the
> Coltrane solo and Philly Joe-Jones swapping fours. And this is a
> guitar player! So, I found I could do it too. I started singing eve-
> rything with him. I mean you're making a horrible noise, it's like
> when people are singing along to their headphones on the subway,
> it's all over the place. It's something where you're not going to read
> a page of music and play it, the era that we came through was not
> about that; you lived it, breathed it, and you felt it. But it was one
> of the most brilliant parts of my education. Terry was amazing to
> teach me that.

With the fuse of passion having been lit by one of the leading jazz musicians in the country, Joy would soon further her studies in a more formal
setting, after she received a phone call from her father who informed her of
a new music course in Jazz that had just begun locally. Having just bought a
beautiful 1956 Selmer Mark VI saxophone and with Bitch no longer active on
the London music scene, she decided to move back to Newcastle and enrol
in the college. Joy admits,

> After hanging out with a top jazz musician who was hailed as the
> best in *DownBeat*, it was obvious to me that I didn't know very
> much. I wanted to be a jazz saxophonist, but I probably sounded
> horrible, though I could read music because I'd had piano lessons.
> So, I arrived late but I was welcomed there, and I managed to stay

a couple of years desperately trying to blow the saxophone and play a little bit of flute. I had a great sax teacher, Brian Whittle, who has since passed away. On my very first day at college, he said, 'come to big band, it's at four o'clock'. So, I showed up at five-past-four and I started to open my case and as I pulled my saxophone out, he said, 'What do you think you're doing?' I replied, 'oh, but you told me to come...' 'Yeah, I told you to come at four o'clock, it's now eight minutes past four. Get out!' And he added that I had missed the bus. Although humiliating, it was a great lesson for a professional life. At one point I was in the sax section playing tenor and we got a new guy in who played tenor and my teacher Brian said, 'He's better than you so we're going to relegate you to baritone'. My teacher was just very straightforward like that. So, I played baritone for about eight months, and I don't know if I told him, but I really enjoyed that, even though it was extremely heavy; I couldn't stand up with it. But you go to college for an education, and I felt like I did do some stuff there though I was absolutely useless at counterpoint, so I gave that up. The education was really there in the things that were important. Brian was all about that whole side of being professional. He told me he admired how I took the baritone and really ran with that. Bob Peacock was the piano and jazz teacher, I remember one time going to his office for a piano lesson and he was in there sitting back with his feet up on the desk listening to Bill Evans and he goes, 'just make yourself comfortable anywhere', and we just carried on listening to the album.

While the college provided plenty of theory, Joy found more practical education whilst working at the Mayfair Mecca Ballroom where she joined the brass section and played six nights a week performing a mix of wartime songs, big band tunes, or pops, depending on the night in question. She says,

It was the only job in town; these places might have started before the war, but they were very much in use throughout the '50s and '60s. They were big ballrooms with a four-piece brass section, John Hedley was the guitar player, and Sting was the bass player, both before I joined along with Mark Wood, who was an incredible genius at twenty years old, he could play any jazz thing in any key, and I ended up living with him. So, I was going to the music college and working, making what seemed at the time to be vast amounts of money for a student, working six nights a week playing saxophone and singing. It was like, 'here's your education!' I mean the music book was so thick, you're just turning pages, blowing, turning pages, blowing, and so on. It was one of those things where you had to wear an evening dress and there were these sections where it said 'soli section' and it meant that you stand up as a group and play together, but I had this one evening dress and I guess I had lost some weight because one night it came time to stand up and the shoulder would drop and the dress would start to fall off and I'm standing there struggling to hold the saxophone and play it. I was making money, but fine evening dresses weren't something I was shopping for.

More work came along for Joy in the form of Red Brass, a ten-piece band with socialist-leaning lyrics out of London, which was attracting the hot young stars of jazz at the time, including trumpeter Dick Pearce, and so Joy left college early to join them. Though how she got the job is not the usual route one takes to securing a position in a modest brass ensemble…

The way I got that gig was pretty extraordinary. Mark Wood, whom I met at The Mayfair Ballroom, was in a band that got a chance to play at what was then a very new jazz festival in San Sebastian. It has since become a very famous jazz festival, but this was 1976 and Herbie Hancock was the main event. So, we drove to San Sebastian where it was raging hot, over a hundred degrees Fahrenheit! We were in the town square and there was all this fast Spanish coming out of loudspeakers; even when we were lying on the beach suddenly Basque/Spanish propaganda would blare out of the loudspeakers, and I couldn't understand what it was saying. I didn't know what the hell was going on. But when it came to the day of playing, we found ourselves in the middle of a Basque uprising! The stage was set up in the ancient town square in front of a big audience, and by now it had reached 105 degrees, I thought my saxophone was going to melt. But I played keyboards, I played saxophone, I sang, and I came off and sat among this group of people who had VIP passes, they were either performers or journalists, and suddenly there was an explosion. Bombs started going off and it was terrifying, so they cordoned-off the square. There was a riot squad with white visors, they looked like something out of *Star Wars*, and we were told that we couldn't move out of the square. We were really scared and holding each other, and the guy I was holding turned out to be the Editor-in-Chief of the *Melody Maker*. But we eventually got out of there and drove home and it took us about three days to get there, but when the next *Melody Maker* came out it had a centre page on the San Sebastian Jazz Festival and there was an entire column about the band and me. The editor had written it, and he was saying, 'watch out for this girl musician, she is in the future, she is amazing'. Someone from Red Brass read that and contacted someone, who gave them a phone number to reach me. Tony, the band leader, asked me to go meet them in London.

This was Joy's second move down to London, but again she didn't stick around. She was in her second year of college and felt that she hadn't yet reached her academic potential, and so she was determined to finish, despite the acclaim from the music press.

> I said, 'I would love to do this but I'm not good enough. I'm not where I want to be. Yes, *Melody Maker* has written me up and I might have something that appeals to some, but I don't have what it takes, I want to take my time in college'. And they said, 'okay, we know who you are, I'm sure we'll be in touch again'. So, I went back to college and had a fabulous second year. Annie Lennox joined Red Brass then, she played flute and sang, but she left a year later and then they called me again. This time I said, 'Yes, I'm ready now!' I only had about three months left of college and in fact the teachers there said, 'You have to go! This is what we all want! You don't need the piece of paper that says you've got a degree. You need this, you need to get the offer'. I took it and played with the band for about eight months.

Following her time with Red Brass, Joy remained in London, where she joined a popular instrumental fusion band called The Jazz Sluts, with whom she would be given ample opportunity to flex her musical muscles. It was through a connection with this group's former keyboardist whom Joy had replaced that her first major professional gig arose. Eye to Eye was a synthpop duo consisting of American singer Deborah Berg and British pianist Julian Marshall, whose shoes Joy was filling in The Jazz Sluts. Eye to Eye was signed to Warner Bros. in the United States and had just recorded their eponymous debut that was produced by Gary Katz, who brought the same kind of slick sophisticated pop sound that he had previously brought to a series of Steely Dan records including *The Royal Scam* (1976), *Aja* (1977), and *Gaucho* (1980). With the duo set to hit the road to promote the record, they needed a keyboard player. It was when Marshall returned to London and caught up with the Sluts and experienced Joy's skills as both keyboardist and vocalist that he considered her as a potential candidate for the upcoming Eye to Eye tour. Several months later Joy got the call to come to America for a proposed three-month tour. Joy recalls,

> They needed a keyboard player and someone who sang, but I also had a synthesizer. If you could play keyboards, play synthesizer, and sing, then you could cover what they would have had to pay two people for. I had a Fender Rhodes, a Mini Moog, and I bought a

Prophet 5 as well. I felt much more like a Prophet person than an Oberheim person. That was my thing. I had a good Fender Rhodes and being in The Jazz Sluts I had to keep playing solos – which I wasn't very good at – but you needed that Rhodes sound to bite because the guitar player was so loud. So, I came over to the US on February 15th, 1982, and I went to the West Village to begin work with Eye to Eye. The first thing I did when I got there was go out to dinner with Donald Fagen because he was involved with Eye to Eye through Gary Katz, who produced Steely Dan. We went into rehearsal in SIR [studio] and Donald happened to be recording *The Nightfly* downstairs. One day I came into rehearsal and my Fender Rhodes was gone! I flipped out and then his road tech came up to me and he says, 'are you Joy?' And I'm still standing there staring at this empty space where my Fender Rhodes previously stood, and he says, 'Oh, Donald has borrowed it, he's looking for a good-sounding Fender Rhodes, so he thought he would try yours because he thought it sounded good'. If you look at the original copies of *The Nightfly* you'll see it says, 'Special Thanks to Joy Askew'. That was about the first thing that happened to me when I arrived in America. I was a huge Steely Dan fan. But Eye to Eye never really got off the ground and got on tour, Warner Bros. decided not to support the band and they pulled the rug out within six weeks. But I earned more money in those six weeks than I had earned in my whole life. They were paying very well. I did not want to leave New York, I still had my visa, and my ticket wasn't for another six weeks, so I went down to Bleecker St. and joined an open mic at Kenny's Castaways at 2 o'clock in the morning, and the guitar player, Larry Saltzman, gave me a phone number and it happened to be a conduit to Joe Jackson.

Indeed, the next major step in Joy's career came about as Joe Jackson was seeking a keyboardist for his 'Night and Day Tour', and specifically a female keyboardist. Released in 1982, *Night and Day* was Jackson's fifth studio album and represented something of a stylistic leap into slicker territory for the former new waver. Several of Jackson's records displayed his considerable chameleonic approach which allowed him to transcend the '80s sonic limitations that trapped so many artists of the time; he crafted musically diverse compositions which often cross genres and production styles within the space of a single song, veering from jazz to new wave to orchestral. On *Night and Day*, the songwriter brought a bright pop production palette to his Cole Porter homage, and such elaborately stylized compositions required an appropriately accomplished ensemble of players to reproduce it on the road. 'I went for the audition and got the gig', Joy confirms.

It was amazing because I felt then that I could live in America, even though we were going off around the world. I think Joe wanted the band to be diverse and being that this was for *Night and Day*, which was his biggest album to date, he didn't want to be behind the keyboards when playing live, he wanted to stand out front, so he brought in a six-piece band for that tour. Sitting behind a keyboard is not the same dynamic for the audience as standing out at the front, so he was looking for two keyboard players and he also had a female percussionist, Sue Hadjopoulos, perhaps also for diversity or because she was a dynamite player! So, we did a little rehearsal at SIR and then went back to England to rehearse for three weeks, and then we were off!

Being part of the Joe Jackson band as he was embracing his greatest commercial success meant for an entirely new experience for Joy, being her first brush with a massive touring and promotional unit, taking her across the globe and into the homes of millions of Americans via *Saturday Night Live*. Joy recalls,

The Joe Jackson tour was a completely different experience altogether. Everybody wanted to know us! The first thing we did was play on the pier in New York on 42nd Street; it was massive, and I had only been in New York for a nanosecond really and here I am on the Hudson River, seeing the sun go down, The Intrepid is there – which is now a museum – and I had more to play and sing than I'd ever performed before. The shows were good, the music was good, and there was all this work to do because we were performing a two-and-a-half-hour show, but you live in the moment. Before we went out to the West Coast to do more concerts out there, we played *Saturday Night Live*. As we walked out on to that stage someone said, 'Forty million!' as in viewers! It was huge. This was the season on which Eddie Murphy was a cast member and blowing up, and Michael Palin was the guest. A friend of mine was there that night because I put her on the guest list and she was wearing a black shiny jumpsuit; I took one look at it and said, 'Give me that. You'll get it back!' and it was all crumpled like she had flown over from London in it, so I took it to the laundry room and while the woman is ironing it Eddie Murphy walks in and starts taking his clothes off (to be ironed) and he's just being him. I was so new to New York I didn't really know who he was beyond that he was on the show. Between me and the laundry girl we made the most of a spirited Eddie Murphy performance. But we [the JJ Band] shot out like a ball from a cannon on that show with such excited energy, so I don't blame anyone for thinking, 'oh my god, these guys are great!' I was playing Hammond Organ and Prophet 5, so it must have looked impressively unusual! Seeing me with those instruments would have been different from seeing me with a piano or acoustic guitar.

Joy continues,

> Joe was immensely popular. The tour was so busy; we travelled across America for five months on a tour bus. I definitely got to see a lot of the country. There were six keyboards on the tour. After the European leg we were asked to play a TV show called *Rockpalast* while we were in Bangkok or Australia, so we'd have to go to Germany to film that and then fly back around the globe to wherever we were. It was all like a very rich dream for a year. He had one song on that tour, 'Everything Gives You Cancer', which is kind of Latin, and Joe sat at the piano to sing that one while the other keyboard player, Ed Roynesdal, and I went out front to play claves and cowbell. I remember drifting off once with the cowbell and I dropped it on the floor. A very loud CLANK! I remember one day in 1982 we played with The Rolling Stones at Roundhay Park – a huge park in Leeds. This was the first of The Stones' big stadium stages, before this they just used venues that were already there, but now they had their own stage with two massive guitars behind at the side of the stage and a crew of two hundred people. The field behind the stage was arranged as a village for the bands, and their part of the village was all Japanese and bamboo, they made a whole deal of it. But that stage was gigantic and at one point when we were playing, Joe shouted to the crowd, 'we're going to take a photograph of you!' and it seems that everybody in the audience took their shirts off. I had gone to Betsy Johnson's shop in SoHo specifically for this Night and Day tour and I bought what was effectively a skating skirt with little pants underneath with a little flare, a bow neck, and long sleeves, and I would wear it with tights and high heels (the early '80s!) So, I was at the back of the stage at the organ, and I had my little skating skirt on, so when I went down to the front of the stage all you could hear was this sea of wolf whistles and then we all took photos.

As Jackson's profile increased and the tour rolled on, it could have easily become a grind for Joy and her bandmates but having a restlessly creative frontman didn't allow for any musical complacency.

> Joe is very inventive. We sang 'Is She Really Going Out with Him' a cappella on the tour. He is still playing it, but differently. He is

never going to repeat himself on tour, he will always do a different arrangement of that song. The thing is, he has to play it, but he is always coming up with new ways of doing things. He looked at me and Sue, and we had other people in the band who sang, so he said we're going to do an a cappella five-part harmony and sang that for the whole tour. (This is on a double album that came out in '86.)

Joy was fresh off the Joe Jackson tour when another crucial career opportunity presented itself. During her brief downtime in New York City, she had been toying around with writing her own material and playing some downtown gigs when she received several calls from the Laurie Anderson camp. Anderson had released her second studio album, *Mister Heartbreak*, in 1984, a record that featured a host of notable collaborators, many of whom Joy would go on to collaborate with in one capacity or another over the ensuing decades, including Anton Fier (of The Golden Palominos), Peter Gabriel, and Phoebe Snow. For the subsequent live shows, which would require some extremely versatile musicians for the complex multimedia production, Anderson's engineer Danny Caccavo and keyboardist and friend Clifford Carter had the right person in mind when they suggested that she hire Joy. 'When I got off the road I wasn't doing that much', she says.

I just writing my own stuff on the porta-studio that I had taken on the road with Joe, and I was kind of diddling around New York meeting people. I was asked to join one band and their drummer was a very, very young Charley Drayton. No one knew who he was at that point. But then I got some calls from Danny and Clifford, who also played with James Taylor for many years and was in the 24th Street Band. The 24th Street Band were pretty well-known when I arrived in NYC, they all knew and played with musicians like Jaco Pastorious, so it was this scene of all musicians who knew each other. But I believe Laurie called Clifford about a keyboard player and he recommended me, so she gave me the job, which was great.

This proved to be a major turning point for Joy as working with the progressively creative and artistically unorthodox Anderson meant embracing all the latest technology available in constructing the kind of multimedia performance art that would constitute a live Laurie Anderson show, which would be captured for posterity on the 1986 concert film *Home of the Brave*. Joy affirms,

I started working with Laurie in 1984 and that was one of the biggest changes that happened with me, it was a major plunge into digital technology. Laurie was way ahead of the curve, whatever it was. She played a Synclavier and was using an original vocoder. On her shows I had a Prophet V, a DX-7, and a Mini Moog. Marcus Miller was down to play bass with us, but at the last minute in rehearsal we learned he couldn't do it, so I had to play bass on the Mini Moog. The DX-7 had just come out, but nothing was MIDI'd. I've got two hands but three keyboards!

Home of the Brave was filmed at Park Theatre in Union City, New Jersey in the summer of 1985 and released the following year. It is as much a visual experience as it is a musical one, with the rear projection footage that provided the backdrop to the stage show displaying symbols – some obvious and some more esoteric – of the themes that inform Anderson's music. Much of the rear-projection footage featured images of mechanical engineering, all oversized, distorted, and repeated for emphatic effect: television screens, airport antennas, boats, and so on, all contributing to a jarringly hypnotic effect when viewed in combination with the band's musical performance. However, technology didn't always save the day, as Joy was to find out upon one particularly memorable wardrobe and instrument issue that occurred in real time onstage. So absurdly humorous was the incident that Anderson scripted the snafu to appear in the filmed concert. As it exists in *Home of the Brave*, Anderson makes a phone call to Joy from the other side of the stage at precisely the moment she is struggling to fix her malfunctioning synthesizer whilst trying to change out of her tutu. Though it is a skit in the film, it did happen for real on a previous night of the tour. Joy recalls,

That was entirely genuine when it first happened. Picture this: we're playing at The Beacon Theatre in New York. I have three keyboards, I have the Prophet, I have the Mini Moog on my left for the bass, and I have the DX-7 on the right. But then suddenly the Prophet, which is the one I'm using the most, the one doing everything, just completely stops working. And it was right before Laurie called me on the phone for this bit. Technology is great but when it doesn't work it's like, 'I don't know!' All I know is the first thing you do is turn it off and turn it back on, but that wasn't working. So, it could have been a cable. I had gotten the tech guys over, and these two guys had come from working with Black Sabbath to Laurie Anderson, they were these tall burly roadies, but they were absolute sweethearts. So, they are fussing around doing their thing and then the phone rings because it's the next part of the show. I'm just supposed to say, 'Hello?' and just listen to her, but I answered the phone and said, 'You know, Laurie, I can't really talk right now. I've got something going on here and I must deal with it'. The audience erupted laughing. The movie version is not as immediate, Laurie wrote me a script, but it was funnier when it was really off the cuff.

So, I just said it as if it was real. Of course, I had lines to learn, and I was sweating buckets, but I think it came off quite funny. Laurie is in the middle of talking about all this incredible stuff, about a half-horse/half-man sort of thing, but when it happened for real, she didn't get that far, I said 'you have to get off the phone! You have to give me space, nothing is working'. But Laurie was superb throughout the whole thing. She is one of the best people I have ever worked with. It was an incredible experience, and especially great to work alongside guitar player Adrian Belew. One time we hooked his guitar up to my Prophet and he started playing, just breakthrough sounds. And I still can't believe I was in a film with William Burroughs! Famous beat poet William Burroughs.

Following her notable stint with Laurie Anderson, Joy would return to her association with Joe Jackson, appearing on the 1986 live album *Big World* (produced by Dave Kershenbaum) and one in which the band made the bold move to perform a set of brand-new songs entirely unfamiliar to the audience. The album's track listing was pulled from across Jackson's five-night residency at New York City's Roundabout Theatre. After that Joy became busy with various other artists and endeavours for several years, including performing with her old hero, Jack Bruce, of Cream. For years, from 1985 to the beginning of 1988, Joy also worked for a jingle house, writing commercials. At that point Joy knew she had to make some money or else face moving home to England, but she felt she had to stay because things were beginning to happen for her. Soon it was becoming obvious that the commercial world was not for her and so she quit after only a couple of years. It was during this period in which Joy became increasingly focused on developing her own work and began to think seriously about pursuing a solo career. However, Joe Jackson would begin recording his tenth studio LP in the winter of 1988, and after being absent for several of his previous records, Joy would return to the Jackson fold once again, convening at Bearsville Studios in the upstate New York town of Woodstock for what would become the *Blaze of Glory* album, which was released to wide acclaim in 1989.

When I came home from the Laurie Anderson Home of the Brave tour I was all fired up because she was so inspiring. The moment I came back I booked a gig at CBGB's for six weeks ahead. I already had some demos and then I wrote a bunch of songs and put a band together in that time. I discovered the benefit of deadlines just from being in and out of America for about a year; I never had deadlines in England, except for my saxophone teacher, I mean that was a deadline because if he said to be there for four o'clock you had to be there at four o'clock. That was a great lesson for me. This was 1985 and a lot of people liked the band I put together, I was told that I was going to get a record deal, and then in 1986, around the time *Home of the Brave* was coming out and when I was about to do *Big World* with Joe Jackson, RCA called up and offered me a development deal. So, I did some songs for that, but it turned out that they wanted me to sound more like Madonna and I didn't understand that. I didn't understand or think of that kind of writing, I was coming from a different point of view. But looking back on it now, I see the legacy of writing is incredible in America and the UK, people really know what they're writing and how to write it. I was just coming out with phrases; I wasn't into lyrics; I didn't even notice a lyric until 1988! I'm really glad that record deal didn't happen, because it wouldn't have been the right kind of thing for me. But by 1988 I felt good about my band, and I had written some songs. My friend Leanne Ungar, who had been the front-of-house engineer for Laurie Anderson, got us some studio time and we went in and cut a four-track EP. That was my first time doing that, and I released it but there was no independent route or internet back then. Then Joe asked me to work on *Blaze of Glory*. That was a whole other album; we went to Bearsville studio in Woodstock and got to experience that Woodstock thing. You really felt the history there. The Band. Dylan, and the people who'd come through the studio. I really loved that experience and Joe was doing a lot of different things with his writing. I sang a duet with him on that album, the single 'Down to London'. I loved that song, I still do. We went back to London to shoot a video for it; it was a great experience. Julian Temple directed. I liked his personality – there was an air of excitement. The place where we shot that video was above a genuine working men's club in North London, next to the canal at the top of Ladbroke Grove. It was so entirely London. All the people in the working men's club were the genuine regulars of the pub, but they had been asked to come in during the daytime and drink and smoke as much as they wanted! We used the hall upstairs that was usually kept for events, and they dressed it up to look like a modern sushi bar. That was my first experience with a big video like that and I loved it.

As the new decade of the 1990s dawned, Joy found herself busy with a variety of projects, from the modest to the massive. In 1991 she toured with Buffalo troubadour and Bruce Springsteen associate, Willie Nile. With a talented band in tow, including erstwhile Suzanne Vega drummer Frank Vilardi, Joy hit the road for what she humorously refers to as 'The Joy and Seven Blokes in a Van Tour'. Joy says,

Willie is a real New York rock 'n' roller, although he is a very diverse musician, but he is very much New York rock, he always wears black. But in '91 they asked me if I would do this tour with him, and I remember times were suddenly very tough that year but Willie's music and Willie himself just made it into a great thing. And the best outcome of that was that I got asked to go up to Woodstock again, to play on a Jules Shear record and this time it was me and thirteen blokes! We were in Dreamland Studio and Stewart Lerman was the producer. One of the guitar players was Steuart Smith, who was also on Willie's tour and has been in The Eagles for the last ten years or so. He was out of Nashville. Tony Levin was the bass player and I really bonded with Tony; we played Scrabble a lot. The way that record went was that we recorded live and then waited until your name got called, and if your name got called it meant you had to go in and re-do your part or an overdub. I was mainly playing Hammond Organ and a little bit of Prophet. Jules Shear writes wonderful, catchy songs. He has written for Cyndi Lauper and The Bangles; many people have recorded his songs, he is a consummate songwriter, and a nice guy.

Having made an impression on Steuart Smith, Joy was asked to meet with country music artist Rodney Crowell. While the Americana aesthetic was something new to Joy, it turned out that those years of studying Jazz and Theory came in handy for the improvisational and structural elements of country performance. 'I had never heard of Rodney', Joy admits, 'but he was very well-known in Nashville'.

He needed a keyboard player to tour a new record that was a different approach for him, for instance several of the tracks were produced by [Joni Mitchell producer] Larry Klein. Steuart asked me if I would come meet Rodney and do the tour. Rodney turned out to be one of the best people I've ever worked with. Me not coming from a country background was exactly what Rodney wanted, he wanted someone who had different influences, coming from outside his usual sound in the band. He told me that his influence was Elvis Presley, and I guess he is always going to have that in him, but he had constructed songs that were arranged outside of the usual country music vernacular. The lyrics were unique, and the production of the record was more expansive than the norm. It was great fun, the rhythm and feel were wonderful, but Rodney would always play these long sets and head into 45 minutes of tunes that I didn't know! There was another keyboard player onstage, Randy Leago and, if I'm being truthful, if I lifted my hands off the keyboard the show wouldn't have stopped, let's put it that way. I had to learn to know what was meant by 44-11-55 – four chord, one chord, five chord. This was how the band would relate the form of a song – there was a lot of 44-11-55 (and other numbers too), because they have two bars of four, two bars of one, and two bars of five, you would just have to know what key you were playing in. That's actually how I was taught in jazz college, except the chords are qualified to be more complex, so I was very comfortable with the way they worked, but suddenly they could just turn around to me and shout 'B Flat!' (letting me know there was an outlier chord in the song). That tour really brought my chops up, I had to really play, play, play; Rodney would shout 'solo!' to me and I would be soloing, even when I didn't know the song!

Soon after that tour ended another opportunity came along, although this time a particularly higher-profile one, thanks once again to Joy's experience with Willie Nile. Bass player Tony Levin called her early one morning with the news that Peter Gabriel had a major tour starting imminently, but he was missing a keyboard player. On the recommendation of Levin and jazz saxophonist Michael Brecker, Gabriel was interested to hear what Joy could bring to his well-oiled machine. So, she duly sent him some recordings of her work and he was suitably impressed, as Joy recalls: 'He called me about a month later from Africa and he left a message on my answering machine; I could just about make out him saying he loved my music amongst all this static and noise from the phone line from Senegal. So, I got hold of a VHS of his previous tour to study all the keyboard parts'. And with that, Joy embarked on Gabriel's mammoth Secret World Tour in support of his 1992 album *Us*. The complex staging of the arena concerts involved a massive rotating video screen, two stages linked by a walkway, multiple moving props, and an army of crew members. This was an elaborate production the size of which was something completely new for Joy, as she remembers:

> We had a square stage and a conveyer belt linked to a round stage which was designed like the sex symbols for female and male joined together. Underneath all this was the underworld, with crew working and a six-screen video lab, but in 1993 it was still somewhat clunky compared to today. We had computers but they were slow, and we didn't have internet. Only Tony Levin and people in the military had internet back then I think! But underneath the stage I had two enormous racks of gear that I called the Twin Towers. We had at least three Prophet Vs rack-mounted (used by PG and myself) and I took my own Prophet and my one-tier Korg Organ. I had to transfer all the keyboard samples over to my Akai samplers, which is what I was using at that point. And I was also using a Korg 88-key, a huge, heavy keyboard that split eight times as a

controller, and it had a little screen on it for multiple pages. So, I had an awful lot of initial setting up to do. It was an amazing, incredible experience, but very, very different from a Joe Jackson or Laurie Anderson tour. The Laurie Anderson tour was on a bus, but she had to have extra people who worked the media stuff because we had reel-to-reel, we had multimedia happening, and we had to have somebody to look after the Synclavier. Some of the crew people were film buffs, so several hours of our days on the bus were spent watching and analysing Orson Welles or Alfred Hitchcock movies. But that was the aesthetic on Laurie's tour, sometimes it was like, 'What are we studying today?' 'Oh, we're analysing the camerawork at the end of *Rear Window*'. I read a lot of books too on the road, I read five books on the film set of *Home of the Brave*, while lying on my back because I didn't want to crumple my dress! Thinking of tours and bands I believe it's important, it's all about the dynamics. On the Joe Jackson tour I don't think he believed what was happening to him on the Night and Day tour, he was going platinum all over the world; we were bouncing around the world. On that tour he would often say to the band, 'let's meet in my room after the gig!' He would have a suite and we would relax and play Scrabble or we would listen to music; we would bring CDs of things we were listening to, being this was before the internet you had to listen to recommendations from other people to discover new music! But on the Peter Gabriel tour, that did not happen. It just wasn't really a social tour. I did play Scrabble with Tony Levin though, as well as a lot of Boggle! We would be playing these games and one time, during an interminably long day waiting at a TV studio, Peter looked over and said, loudly, 'what are you guys doing?!' I was very content passing the time playing word games – still am! That tour was a bit scattered, and I didn't understand the dynamic. I could understand the work with Laurie Anderson, and I could understand the Joe Jackson tours, a lot better. It was all about music or about film and music. We were swapping cassettes and listening to music together and all that kind of thing. The Rodney Crowell tour embraced hiking! (We were driving backwards and forwards across the Rocky Mountains a fair bit.) I learned a lot and I heard a lot of stuff. In fact, on one of the Joe Jackson tours in 1989, we were on the bus, and he had the score to *The Rite of Spring* and he challenged us to follow the score! Steve Elson, baritone saxophone player, and I followed the score while it played on the [bus] speaker! He and I followed it page-by-page, but even when it got into things like that, it was about music; but the Peter Gabriel tour was not so much, except for Peter himself who spent time listening to my songs with me and giving me extremely helpful suggestions that I still think about today! I left the tour after about eight months and after that everything was different, I had to learn how to diversify.

The time, it seemed, was finally right for Joy to make her solo career a priority. Having written a collection of songs on a reel-to-reel 8-track over the course of a year and a half, she proceeded to obtain a record deal with the help of her friend, the producer and multi-instrumentalist, Larry Klein. The result is *Tender City*. Released in 1996, the album is produced by Joy and mixed by Mike Shipley, whose considerable credits include engineering albums for The Cars, Def Leppard, Joni Mitchell, and Tom Petty and the Heartbreakers. Joy says,

> Sadly, Larry did not produce the record, but he played on it, and he brought in Mike to mix it. Larry had worked with Mike quite a bit, who came in after we bumped up my 8-track recordings to 24 tracks. The record label, Private Music – who were on BMG – liked the demos so much that they wanted to keep them. A lot of what is on the album is there from the original demos. There is a song called 'Cool Water' and most of that is from the 8-track. We went into Clubhouse Recording Studio in upstate NY and the label was extremely worried about the bump up to 24 tracks. At that point I knew enough about technology, and so did the people I was working with, to say, 'Well, that's a no-brainer, you just run the track from the tape!' You only had seven tracks of music on an 8-track reel-to-reel, so you just run tracks one to seven on the 24-track. It was fine, there was nothing that was going to go wrong with that; the thing that was difficult about that record was we were literally adding drums last, which is kind of unusual. But I got to meet Jerry Marotta, he played on three of the tracks; Shawn Pelton came in and worked on a few tracks also, adding some big drums, I mean that is a strange way to do it, but they liked the songs and came in and did a great job! Peter Gabriel sang on one song; he was skiing in the Alps, but he had his VHS recorder with him, so he was able to record his voice part and we flew it in – we were beginning to get into this technology that was still basic in comparison to what is normal today.

Joy continues,

> The head of Private Music, Ron Goldstein, was a jazz fan, he would talk about jazz musicians with me and would go see some shows together. So, we had a good context in which to connect. When I met Ron, who was someone I would end up being friends with, it was a delight because we had a lot in common. Ron was close

friends with Ry Cooder, who I think is amazing and someone with a really distinctive sound, that which has been in my life for fifty years! When I was seventeen or eighteen, I had Ry Cooder's *Into the Purple Valley*. So, we tried to get Ry to play on the record but instead we got Greg Leisz, who played a lap steel; he is a great player. It's sad that *Tender City* didn't go anywhere commercially, but I thought it was going to have some success, because I got such great reviews, and then nothing really happened. Ron was about to sign what became the Buena Vista Social Club, that would be produced by Ry Cooder, and then BMG dissolved the Private Music label as it was and merged it with another label, I guess not realizing Buena Vista Social Club was poised to become this big musical event that it became! It was interesting because it was a small label where everybody knew everybody; the photoshoot was a miracle, I loved the cover, I loved the Art Designer, I even went out and stayed in her house. The A&R man and I would talk all the time. We all knew each other like that. Private Music paid for some demos for what would have been my next release but then the label was over, so I just used the demos for a second EP that I released on my own. But they sound like demos. It is wonderful when you do have a good experience!

With *Tender City* released but with its author in limbo following the demise of her record label, Joy continued to perform in downtown NY, playing at the likes of the newly established Arlene's Grocery, a modest music bar on the Lower East Side which was operated in its earliest incarnation by Irishman Shayne Doyle after the closure of his hip hangout Sin-é. But there was one evening at Arlene's that proved particularly important for Joy; while the regulars of Arlene's were there to enjoy Joy's performance, she knew she was playing to anything but a regular audience; in fact, she would be performing something of a showcase for one of the music industry's most respected executives, Quincy Jones. Joy had signed a publishing deal with Warner Chappell, who were associated at that time with Quincy Jones Publishing. As it turned out, those couple of years writing jingles were not time and effort spent in vain.

How Quincy Jones signed me was this: Judith Bright, Quincy's head of publishing, had heard a song demo that I had originally begun writing for a jingle. It had this quirky little chorus, and she sang it to him down the phone! He was in Paris, and she said, 'I think you should sign this girl', and after she sang him my song on the phone to Paris he said, 'Yes, sign her!' Consequently, I never recorded that song. Flash-forward to 1997. The Lower East Side was starting to open up. Jeff Buckley had already done his thing at

Sin-é and Shayne had opened Arlene's Grocery, so this was the very beginning of the club and I had played there in its first few weeks. This was the Lower East Side and it looked like shit, or perhaps you might think it looked great, but at that time it looked like an area of New York you wouldn't want to go to at night. There was nothing else around, except for one Mexican restaurant opposite, The Sombrero. So, we sat in there, in The Sombrero, me and the rep from Quincy Jones Publishing and the rep from Warner Chappell waiting for Quincy's car to arrive. Quincy Jones himself was coming down to see me play! And this was a moment I will never forget – he arrived at the club, but the place was full! They managed to get him a seat at the front of the house by offering someone a bottle of whiskey to give up their seat. I have to say that he is incredible. I was totally enamoured in being one of his writers, but I don't think I really took advantage of it as much as I could have. I remember being in London in the '70s and buying Quincy's album, *Body Heat* and Michael Jackson's *Off The Wall* and just playing them over and over again on my little turntable, and there he is standing outside Arlene's Grocery shaking my hand and giving me a hug.

Looking back at the industrial context of the mid- to late 1990s, the time in which it seemed that female artists were finding a platform in mainstream musical genres, notably the well-produced folk genre in which the likes of Indigo Girls, Natalie Merchant, Suzanne Vega succeeded, it seems that *Tender City* was just too elusive to define, too broad in its musical aesthetic, too wonderfully colourful and textural across its twelve tracks for the media to pigeonhole Joy into the limiting identifier of 'singer-songwriter', a label that was being applied to many of the successful female solo artists of the period. But while neither *Tender City* nor Joy fit with any pre-conceived commercial models, the atmosphere was right for her to take part in what would become an annual celebration of female artists. Lilith Fair is the brainchild of Canadian musician Sarah McLachlan, who conceived the event as a touring festival which programmes female solo artists as well as bands that boasted women singers. The first tour took place in 1997 and featured Sheryl Crow, Tracy Chapman, and Emmylou Harris, as well as the three acts mentioned above. Making an appearance on the Village Stage at the festival's debut was Joy Askew.

The term 'singer-songwriter' was not around when I first played at CBGB's, there was no singer-songwriter terminology; they wouldn't call Jimi Hendrix a singer-songwriter, or Sting. The label came in with this folk revival, but I would say to people, 'I'm not a singer-songwriter!' That was for Suzanne Vega and her well-channelled domain, and she's got that, but I felt I wasn't like that because I was coming from a wider and different musical scope; I was in The Jazz Sluts for god's sake! Solo after solo! But that was the musical landscape of the time, and it wasn't me. Though after *Tender City* and after my first deal fell through, I did get to go on the Lilith Fair tour for a week and it was fantastic, so different from the many festival stages that I had done up to that point with Peter Gabriel or Joe Jackson or any of these male artists. Now it was a women's thing and even though I was on the tiniest stage I felt it was something great to be involved in for that week, and I noticed how there had been a musical shift, and music shifts all the time, but I really noticed the change then. This was '97, and it wasn't really to do with technology as we know it now, but it was just that the younger generation had truly arrived, and it was going to sound different. So, listening at Lilith Fair was the first time I really felt that, but that was when I was launching out there determined to be an artist as opposed to always working for other people. Fiona Apple was one of the headliners and I got to see her three or more times. Tracy Chapman was there for a week as well, obviously Sarah McLachlan was there for the whole tour, and I got to see Emmylou Harris. But on the B-Stage across from us was a band called Once Blue and that was Jesse Harris and Rebecca Martin, and it was Jesse who later helped Norah Jones to success because he wrote most of the songs on her first album. Prior to this I wasn't really having girlie experiences in New York, I don't know how else to put it, but it was all male bands. There might be another girl in the band, but they were all very male-oriented. You had Michael Jackson and his female guitarist, Jennifer Batten, and Prince had Rosie Gaines, Wendy and Lisa and Sheila E, David Bowie had Gail [Ann Dorsey] and Joe Jackson worked with Sue Hadjopoulos for many years, that kind of thing. I was very conscious at certain times that it was still a man's world. It was very rare indeed, I'm probably a bit guilty of it myself in terms of when I did the *Queen Victoria* album with the big brass band, somebody said to me 'why don't you hire women for this?' and I said, 'men and women are not on my mind here, brass are on my mind and I've managed to get the best brass band in England, so I'm not going to question if there are any females in there'. And as it happened, there were women in the brass band! There are some great female players, but it is still rare. At the time when Lilith Fair happened it felt to me like something was opening up more for female artists. Suddenly on Lilith Fair you were getting to know other women musicians. Even though I was a small part of it, it was kind of a mound or a peak in time, it was a bit different.

Joy has continued to release an eclectic body of solo works and collaborations. Her albums, including *The Pirate of Eel Pie* (2008), *Drunk on You* (2011), *Queen Victoria* (2017), and *Everything Is Different* (2022) display Joy's distinct songwriting prowess and comprehensive command of musical styles. Meanwhile she has engaged with successive generations of significant singers and songwriters, including Sufjan Stevens, Cat Martino, James Maddock, and Takuya Nakamura, who have all benefitted from the vast musical canvas that Joy can provide. The experience has been pedagogically reciprocal and mutually beneficial for all involved. Joy says,

> I joined a women's choir [Indie Brooklyn musicians] about twelve years ago, and it was really the idea of a singer, Cat Martino, who is a Brooklyn indie musician, who I have known for a long time. She is always full of ideas but then the practicalities have to take shape. When she suggested the choir, I thought that it was a great idea, so she called a load of girl singers she knew and we convened and she shared some ideas of doing Benjamin Britten and some of those songs that are seasonal, kind of a Christmas thing. But it was very scattered in the beginning, we were sitting there trying to sing and someone says, 'you know, we need a conductor,' and then everybody looked at me! And I'm like, 'What? I don't know how to do that!' I was way older than everybody else there, so I guess they felt like I must be the one. So, then I got very excited at the thought of conducting and I ended up looking at YouTube for ideas and I thought, 'Okay, this is really confusing!' But I said I would do it, and because Cat is very well-connected to a more modern era of musicians we got off to a very good start and we managed to get into a beautiful historic church every year in Brooklyn Heights, Plymouth Church. It's from the 1600s or 1700s, [George] Washington was there, it was important in the colonial days, and it became very important for the underground railroad in Slave times. The people who run it now are very nice and accommodating to us. But I think anybody who is a proper conductor or someone from a proper choir would probably laugh at me, but we have a lot of fun. I found out from doing it that I had been missing something from my approach to music: what the intent is. This choir is the same thing, you've got to hold on to excellence but at the same time you've got to be there in the moment. A lot of the singers change every year, so I never know everybody's name, and nearly all of the singers are half my age. But that's a big joy for me being involved in something like that, because their take on music is so different from everything that I have dragged up behind me from the '60s.

Joy continues,

> I got to work with Sufjan Stevens through Cat, she sang with him for quite a while. It was for Sufjan's album *All Delighted People*. There were twelve or thirteen singers, and we went into a church here in Brooklyn starting around January 2nd, 2010, and it was freezing cold, I remember because we all had our big jackets on and hats. Sufjan really is an incredible example of an indie musician with the way he recorded all the choral sections onto his laptop in four or five days. We would rehearse, record, rehearse, record, and he would move us around the church, and at one point the sopranos were so loud that he put them up in a pulpit in the other end of the church. He only used the natural reverb of the church on the recording. It sounds absolutely incredible. I was inspired to be there!
>
> James Maddock is someone I met a long time ago, in 1998 when he was in the band Wood. They came over from England and got a record deal with Columbia Records and when they realized they needed a keyboard player somebody from the label called me and asked if I would go down to Philadelphia and play on the album. They said the music had a Bruce Springsteen kind of sound and I just loved the piano playing on Springsteen's records, it was that development of the classic rock style of playing. I got down there to meet them, and they were very interesting lads from Leicester! They had that rustic Americana kind of sound, but it's Americana-English or something, it's that kind of thing where you have an interesting blend of stuff. I could tell the songs would be memorable. Since then, James and I have kept up and for the last five years we've lived around the corner from each other, and he is on quite a few of my latest album's tracks.

In 2002, Joy took her love of jazz and infused it with the hip drum 'n' bass sounds that were emerging from British cultural hotspots like Bristol which were making their way over to New York at the turn of the millennium. Feeling restless as the music underground was thriving downtown, Joy would make some late-night/early morning visits to the clubs to catch some of the likes of Nerve, the experimental improvisational project of virtuoso drummer Jojo Mayer which featured, among others, multi-instrumentalist Takuya Nakamura. A chance meeting with Takuya in a nearby diner led to the recording of an excellent downtempo jazz electronica album that the pair released under the moniker of Echo. Joy says,

This sound that was coming out of England with the likes of the Asian Dub Foundation began to make its way over to New York around 1999 and I started to really dig it. I would get in a cab or go on the subway all the way downtown to this gig that was starting at one o'clock in the morning. I discovered Jojo Mayer's band Nerve. Takuya Nakaura was in the band, Tim Lefevbre was on bass sometimes, and there was a guy named Roli Mosimann mixing them. It was like hearing the Miles Davis album *Jack Johnson* for the first time. It was new and original. It was so good! And then I happened to be in a diner one night and Takuya was there; I recognized him from Nerve. So, when he walked past me, I just said, 'hey, you!' and made him sit down and talk to me; and then we ended up saying we would do something together. So, we did what we described as 'putting our two samplers together'. I had an Akai S5000 and he had a Roland SP. He played me this percolating loop and I started singing 'I've Got You Under My Skin' over the top of it, because that's what it reminded me of, something bubbling under the skin, and we recorded it in twenty minutes. But at that time, Takuya was a Japanese guy with a laptop, ahead of the curve, making fast decisions and he would do the editing in no time, it was so modern, and he taught me how to do that in a way. With the samplers I felt that I could do anything I wanted. I went over to digital in my studio around this time; although I'd had a digital tape recorder before that, I went completely onto Digital Performer.

Soon enough, the duo signed a record deal with New Line Cinema and hit the road, touring the US and opening for former Talking Head, David Byrne, in the UK and Ireland.

It was all very, very exciting. We had Mark Wood with us, the young jazz guitar player I lived with back in college, he joined Echo and the three of us made a big noise. I used a Korg Kaoss Pad and would do a kind of tactile thing with my fingers on it while I was playing and that speaks to me much more than the things where you have to program something in. So, I was swooping up and down on that pad as well as singing and playing keyboards. Takuya had a whole rig with electronic drums, trumpet and keyboards.

For *The Pirate of Eel Pie* and *Drunk on You* Joy hooked up with renowned South African-English multi-instrumentalist Ricky Fataar, known for his work with The Beach Boys, Bonnie Raitt, and Boz Scraggs, among others. Joy previously met Fataar through a mutual friend, Tom Waits's guitarist Marc Ribot, who recommended Joy for an album that Fataar was producing in New York City after witnessing her live at CBGB's. After getting acquainted with Fataar the pair worked together on the 1989 Phoebe Snow record, *Something Real*, at The Power Station studio in Manhattan.

> After we did the Phoebe Snow record, we kind of kept up with each other. When I was on the Peter Gabriel tour I called him up because we were going to San Francisco, and I knew he had moved there. So, he took me over to Bonnie Raitt's house, over the Golden Gate Bridge. It was amazing to meet her and have dinner. I invited her to the Peter Gabriel concert the next day and then afterwards we hung out and at one point she said, 'You've got to show me what you're doing!' They hadn't dismantled the stage at this point, so I brought her out and showed her the underworld of the stage with all my racks and my twin towers. She is a very inspiring person; her voice is incredible. And then Ricky built a studio in Berkeley, so I went out there and started recording tracks with him for what would become *The Pirate of Eel Pie*. Ricky co-produced that with me, we recorded that in 2005 and it came out in 2006. The last time I saw Ricky and Bonnie was when they were on tour with James Taylor. Ricky is an iconic drummer, but apart from that he can play a lot of instruments, he is one of those geniuses. I love *The Pirate of Eel Pie*, and I don't want to say I love my own records, but it really represents a time when I was more in San Francisco and had a different feel of everything. After that I went on to *Drunk on You* which basically happened here in New York because people were listening to my band and saying to me, 'you should just record this band live', because it sounded so good. A very sad thing happened with the song 'Had a Bad Day' from that record, and it is due to the fact that I don't have a manager or anybody looking after me who are in the know. I put it out through CD Baby and signed onto all the electronic/streaming outlets and then I started receiving money every month, which is very unusual for someone like me. I didn't know that I could actually go and check the specs of the song to see how it was doing, so I just thought the money was coming from the few albums I had on there, but in fact it was coming from one song in particular! That was 'Had a Bad Day'. What happened was it had made it onto a playlist that I had no idea about, I had no idea what a fucking playlist was, nor did anybody who knew me! It had tens of thousands of plays in a very short time. Through a well-intentioned offer from a friend to sign a distribution deal, believing this would be a better offer, the album *Drunk On You* came off the CD Baby platform and I lost that particular playlist advantage I'd had. An example of fast-changing times… and me not keeping up!

In recent times, Joy has continued to play shows in New York City whilst engaging in educating future generations of musicians and drawing out the musical potential of others through her involvement in songwriting groups. It is through these sessions that she has been able to offer insights on understanding and appreciating the complex history of music as well as practical advice gleaned from so many years as a professional studio and touring musician. And like any good curator of an artform, she is introducing and directing people to important and influential artists, putting the music they are learning into the context of the time and place of the artists who composed it. For Joy, this kind of historical context, as well as the ability to consider the time and place of our own lives in which we hear our favourite music, is as crucial a key as any theoretical discipline in understanding the music that we love to listen to.

> It is much more of a songwriters' hangout than it is a workshop, but it's a joint effort on the part of whoever is there, as in there is nobody in particular running it. It really helped everybody during the pandemic, just having a togetherness with people that you know. It got to the point where writers were asking if we could Zoom in every two weeks. Instead of having to cope with everything that goes with being in lockdown, we could enter this world of music. I have to say that the younger generation are so masterful at such a young age, and so capable of really getting into lyrics, dissecting and asking questions, and critiquing in a very positive way; they come up with such unique stuff. I always say, 'Don't fall into the easiest thing, into a known category'. Intent is very important. When I was teaching one day, a student said he was listening to the composer Steve Reich and so I told him to look up Phillip Glass as well, because when you get to him you will discover a contemporary, and go listen to others like Eno, and then go back and listen to *Tubular Bells* because that was very breakthrough. It's all about perception, the perception of music. Usually as an artist you are off on your own individual journey and you are just seeing what's in front of you when you are working, but I felt that in the last few years, and especially now during the pandemic and teaching college, I've felt that students are really there to explore and basically it gives me the opportunity to revisit and try to reimagine things that I maybe didn't have the time or wherewithal to imagine before. Putting music history and artists into context is interesting because you can see how people approach the material differently with or without context. I'll ask my students to sing a song but to me they're not picking up on the intent of the song, they're picking up on something else. When they sing 'Sitting on the Dock of the Bay' by Otis Redding or 'What's Going On?' by

Marvin Gaye, it's not that I want them to copy the original artist in style, I never want them to do that, but to find the intent of the song. But obviously they're not feeling the same thing because they weren't around when these songs came out. But then again, is that really relevant? Because none of us were around in Mozart's time. I am fascinated by what it is we hear when we listen to music and it's such an individual thing. Perhaps that is my next step, to think about what we hear when we listen to music and to make myself hear more or differently. If you were somewhere when a really big song came out it carries certain contexts. Some songs can carry all these personal memories, feelings, and visuals for us as individuals. But it's also a collective thing with your friends, family, and anybody else in your country who was around when that song hit, it means there was a collective experience. And it also places the artist in context because it makes you consider where they were at that time in their career and how they delivered that song to you. I find it to be very fascinating. Regarding the fifty-five or sixty years of this era of pop music, I don't know if it has ever been talked about in this way. And I don't know how valid that question is because I could also ask myself what do I feel when I listen to music? Maybe all the questions are valid.

Joy continues,

I do think good songs can go to a lot of different voices, but what I have noticed is that understanding where the song comes from is what eludes a lot of people. I had a big struggle with my voice, I still do, but I know I have some go-to places that I can reach and which I've been teaching to other people for a long time, but one thing my teacher said to me was that you sing on vowel sounds. Anything goes in pop music and in rock, but basically your voice is a vowel sound, so I went back and took four terms of studying Sanskrit, which is thought to be the first language. One of the things they taught was that one vowel leads into the next shape and so on, which is a really amazing teaching tool. Another thing I learned was something called Nada Yoga, which says that every person's body has a vibration, and this changed me, because I started thinking about it. Your vibration is the note that feels so natural it sings itself and you realize that we're dealing with soundwaves here, the vibration of the note within your body. If somebody wants to sing 'Driver's License' by Olivia Rodrigo by copying her sounds or launch into 'Hallelujah', are they really thinking about the vibration that Leonard Cohen was on because that was damn tremendous with that deep voice! So, I'm very much into that and into the intent as you go to sing, what is going on before you take the breath, they are the main things for me. Joni Mitchell had it especially when she was writing and writing, and her voice would just ring out. On *The Last Waltz* she sings 'Coyote' as if it's not difficult. I was fortunate to perform at a concert in 1999 at the Central Park Summer Stage that was called 'Joni's Jazz' and she actually came to it. Chaka Khan was one of the artists, so was Annie Ross and Jon Hendricks. I sang a duet with Joe Jackson, 'Down To You', and at the last minute I was asked to sing 'Coyote' and with that fantastic song we're talking lyrics upon lyrics. The band was a 16-piece headed up by Vernon Reid from Living Colour and I got through the song and enjoyed it tremendously! But then I'm watching *The Last Waltz* again and I see Joni perform it and it is frickin' effortless, but she wrote it in her vibration, she wrote in a place where she was singing on the wave. So, if you are trying to do somebody else's song it might not always happen, you have to bring it into your own being.

There have been many turning points throughout Joy Askew's fifty-year career, so much so that there is a song on her latest album called 'The Turning Point'. But just what are some of those crucial moments?

Turning points... that's a really good question! The last eighteen months that we have been through [in the pandemic] has really got me thinking about my life the way it is now. Once technology hit, things started to change incredibly and I remember Jerry Marotta saying that he used to do one thing – that thing being he was the iconic drummer for Peter Gabriel, but then he said, '...now I'm having to do many different things!' So, turning points, yes, they are those things I mentioned, such as Quincy Jones signing me; my first record deal and Larry Klein, just by force of his presence, convincing people that they are going to want this. Another one was Joe Jackson turning to me in the audition to be keyboard player on his next tour in 1982 (after me only being in New York for a few weeks) and saying, 'do you know *Night and Day*?' – and of course I did, because I went to jazz college and it's what you play when you are working in piano bars! – and when we got to the bridge he turned to me and said, 'do you want the gig?' Things like that are a major turning point. Another big moment for me was when my friend from England, Mark Saunders, came over to the US. He had produced Tricky and Cyndi Lauper and we became friends when he married a friend of mine, Sue Cirillo. Sue and Mark formed a commercial company, and he called me one day after I came back from the Peter Gabriel tour and asked me, 'Do you know about Nusrat Fateh Ali Khan and can you sing like him?' I said, 'Yes, I know who he is, and in fact I have been practising trying out that kind of sound!' So, he asked me to come in and sing something like that and so I did, we replaced his samples of Nusrat with my own phrases and we forgot about it. Then about three years later he called me up in a slight panic at 9am and asked if I could get down to the studio immediately. He had lost (erased by mistake?) my vocal stripe and needed me to do that again. The note that I had to hit was a High D in a chest voice going up to an E Flat, singing a weaving melody before I reached up to that point. He said it was for a very big opportunity, but he needed that vocal stripe so that he could show the agency different versions. So, I just got the coffee on, put on my coat with my pyjamas still on I think, got down to the studio in Midtown, and I recorded it very quickly in about ten or fifteen minutes because the clients were on the way! And we won the jingle, which played a lot, and I bought a house in France! Mark Saunders is an excellent musician/producer and has mixed the first song on the record that I'm making now, 'Diaries'.

The past year of the pandemic has been such a space for reckoning and thinking and I feel I am in a different place as a songwriter right now. I'm excited for the future and I'm so aware of wanting to move forward and sometimes I'm concerned about not sounding dated. Although I don't think I should be focusing on it in that way! You wonder if you are going down a rabbit hole, and maybe sometimes that is necessary, if you are finding something is working for you and you keep honing in and focusing on that. I'm sure these questions go on in the minds of a lot of artists and writers, but there are no rules or set patterns, it's entirely open, which is a beautiful thing. I'm so lucky to be still doing all this!

Figure 1: Gail Ann Dorsey in the studio.
Courtesy of Gail Ann Dorsey Collection. Photo by Tom Eberhardt-Smith

Figure 2: Gail Ann Dorsey, performing live.
Screengrab. *A Reality Tour* (2004 film)

Figure 3: Gail onstage with David Bowie, at The Point Theatre, Dublin, Ireland.
Screengrab. *A Reality Tour* (2004 film)

Figure 4: Clare Kenny portrait.
Courtesy of Clare Kenny Collection

Figure 5: Sinead O'Connor (left) sings with Clare Kenny.
Screengrab. Leverkusener Jazztage (2007 WDR television broadcast)

Figure 6: Clare performing live.
Courtesy of Clare Kenny Collection

Figure 7: Tracy Wormworth performing as part of The B-52s.
Lawrence Brownlee. ©Lawrence Brownlee

Figure 8: Sting (left) with Tracy, live in São Paulo, 1987.
Maristela Collucci. ©Maristela Colucci

Figure 9: Tracy playing bass for renowned American saxophonist Wayne Shorter. Screengrab. Leverkusener Jazztage (1990 television broadcast)

Figure 10: Sara Lee lost in the groove, live onstage with Gang of Four. Courtesy of Sara Lee Collection. Photo by Steve Cross

Figure 11: Sara Lee performing live with The Thompson Twins
Courtesy of Sara Lee Collection. Photo by Susan Alzner

Figure 12: Sara on tour in the 1980s.
Courtesy of Sara Lee Collection. Photo by Susan Alzner

Figure 13: Sara entertaining the crowd.
Courtesy of Sara Lee Collection. Photo by Susan Alzner

Figure 14: Joy Askew performs.
Cristina Arrigoni. ©Cristina Arrigoni

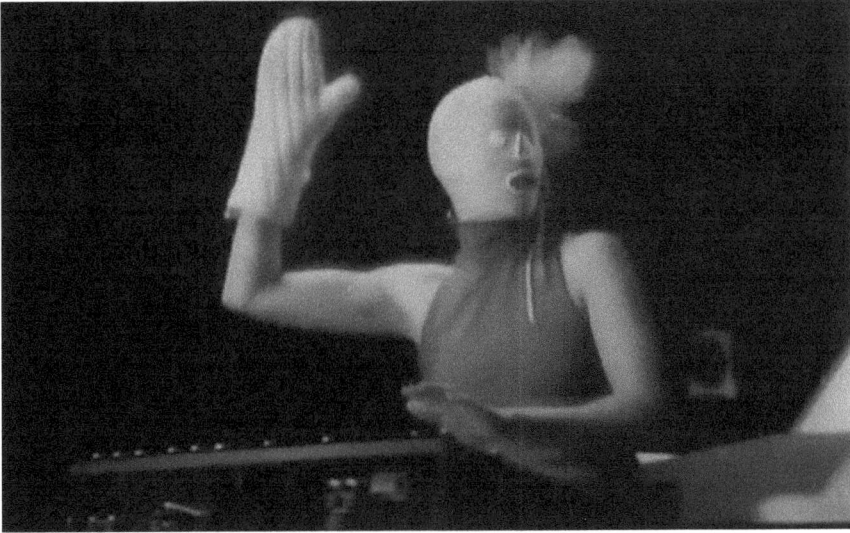

Figure 15: Joy joins in the sartorial fun filming Laurie Anderson's *Home of the Brave*. Screengrab. *Home of the Brave* (1986 film)

Figure 16: Joy in Germany, playing live with Joe Jackson. Screengrab. *Joe Jackson: Live at Rockpalast* (1983 film)

Figure 17: Joy providing keys and backing vocals for Laurie Anderson. Screengrab. *Home of the Brave* (1986 film)

Figure 18: Susan Miller, onstage at the All Quiet on the Western Front festival in Oakland, California, 1981. Courtesy of Susan Miller Collection

Figure 19: Tanks band photo, featuring Susan Miller (left).
Courtesy of Susan Miller Collection

Figure 20: Frightwig on tour.
Courtesy of Susan Miller Collection

Figure 21: Frightwig band photo, 1986.
Courtesy of Susan Miller Collection. Photo by Bobby Castro

Figure 22: Caroline Dale rehearsing with The Royal Philharmonic Orchestra for the Concert for Care, 18 October 2010.
©Alamy

Figure 23: Caroline performing live.
Courtesy of Caroline Dale Collection

Figure 24: Caroline recording.
Courtesy of Caroline Dale Collection

Figure 25: Caroline onstage with David Gilmour at the Robert Wyatt-curated Meltdown festival in London, 2001.
Screengrab. *David Gilmour in Concert* (2002 film)

Figure 26: Angie Pollock with The Lightning Seeds.
Screengrab. *TFI Friday* (1997 television broadcast)

Figure 27: Angie in the studio during the making of Tanita Tikaram's 2016 album, *Closer to the People.*
Courtesy of Angie Pollock Collection

Figure 28: Angie Pollock, Emily Dolan Davies, and Amanda Kramer, on tour with Tom Bailey.
Courtesy of Amanda Kramer Collection

Figure 29: Angie rehearsing for an upcoming tour with Peter Gabriel.
York Tillyer ©York Tillyer

Figure 30: Lori Barbero performing with Babes in Toyland at the 1993 Reading Festival.
Screengrab. Reading Festival (1993 television broadcast)

Figure 31: Lori in front of the star wall at the legendary First Avenue, Minneapolis.
Angela Boatwright. ©Angela Boatwright

Figure 32: Lori drums and sings with the reformed Babes in Toyland at Primavera Sound,
Spain, 2015.
Screengrab. *Babes in Toyland: Live at Primavera* (2015 television broadcast)

Figure 33: Sue Hadjopoulos appears in Cyndi Lauper's music video for 'What's Going On'. Screengrab. *What's Going On* (1986 music video)

Figure 34: Sue poses with her instruments.
Courtesy of Sue Hadjopoulos Collection

Figure 35: Sue onstage with Cyndi Lauper.
Courtesy of Sue Hadjopoulos Collection

Figure 36: Sue sings and provides percussion for Cyndi Lauper in Yokohama.
Screengrab. *Cyndi Lauper Live in Yokohama* (1991 video recording)

6 Sara Lee

Amid the Covid-recovering concert economy of 2022, it was announced that Britain's post-punk agitators Gang of Four were reforming and hitting the road in celebration of a newly released boxset of their earliest material. That they were doing so in the absence of recently deceased guitarist Andy Gill made some question the decision: would they succeed without his unique style of playing? But there was also cause for celebration by those who discovered the band during their commercial peak with the albums *Songs of the Free* (1982) and *Hard* (1983), for this was the period that enthusiasts of those records will recognize as 'The Sara Lee Years'. Indeed, the eminent bassist was returning to the band to which she had brought her skilfully percussive funk-infused aesthetic and background singing which exquisitely supported Jon King's sprechgesang vocal style. So, this reunion wasn't just a meaningful act for admirers of the band, but for the bassist herself, as for the past thirteen years she has decidedly remained off the road after twenty-seven years of tour-bussing around the world with artists as diverse as The B-52s, Indigo Girls, Ani DiFranco, and The League of Gentlemen, as well as many others. Having played with a roster of acts as varied as those mentioned, it is a surprise that Sara's musical upbringing wasn't as variegated as the trajectory of her career. Having been brought up in a classical environment, Sara was unfamiliar with the popular genres of the day. But as with many musicians featured in this book, to whom the time and place of their musical awakenings were as important as any formal education, Sara's entry into the music industry is no less temporally fortuitous.

With punk having exploded and subsequently imploded by the early 1980s, the so-called 'post-punk' movement arose, bringing some production polish and more elaborate musicality to the socio-political themes of its generic predecessor; it was within this environment that Sara's unique style would be discovered and utilized to great effect, beginning with King Crimson guitarist Robert Fripp's short-lived experimental project, The League of Gentlemen. The eponymous record that the group made in 1980 features an unorthodox and musically sophisticated hybrid of danceable prog-infused art-rock that would have listeners in no doubt as to the talents of the bassist laying the low-end foundation for Fripp's prodigious noodling and erstwhile XTC songwriter Barry Andrews's keyboard playing. While Fripp and Andrews were accomplished players of many years, Sara was relatively new to her instrument, having only picked up the bass guitar three years prior. Though having been born into a musical milieu meant for an early immersion into the world of harmony and melody that would serve her well when sharing the stage with well-established artists.

The Lee household in Hereford was one in which music abounded thanks to Sara's parents being educators of the art. At the age of ten, Sara took to the timpani, playing in orchestras and engaging in her classical studies just as the countercultural movement of the British Invasion was exploding across the country. Informed by the American delta blues, this new brand of English rock'n'roll raged across the radio waves of the mid-1960s, but it was Debussy and Shostakovich, rather than The Stones and The Beatles, who provided the soundtrack to Sara's childhood and adolescence. However, in just a few years the dual culture shock of Ozzy Osbourne and James Brown would awaken the youth to the sounds of something new.

> I didn't listen much to anything else until I was fourteen when I was given my first LP, which was the debut Black Sabbath album. Another early record of mine was Emerson Lake and Palmer's *Tarkus*. Maybe because of my orchestral experience I enjoyed the more complex 'prog rock' as opposed to 'plain old' Beatles pop songs, as I thought of them at the time. Although I do remember at the age of nine, working out 'Fool on the Hill' with my best friend on our recorders!

> I grew up in a family full of classical musicians, my parents were music teachers, so I had nothing but classical music around me. At ten years old I started playing in orchestras, my first instrument was timpani which I loved, then double bass.

A few years later at the age of sixteen, Sara began attending a Friday night disco in a Hereford youth hostel, and it was here that she began to be exposed to a whole other world of music the likes of which she had never experienced before. 'It really started there. I discovered James Brown's 'Sex Machine' and thought it was the best thing I'd ever heard'.

Being born to pedagogical parents it was fully expected that Sara would follow suit. However, not being naturally inclined to academia meant her entry to university-level musical education was prohibited. 'I failed to graduate', she admits, and what that means is that I did not finish high school. My mum and dad fully expected that I would become a music teacher, but I failed everything at school. I wanted to be a professional timpanist, but because I failed at high school I could not get into college, and you couldn't become a timpanist in an orchestra if you didn't go to college… unless you were a prodigy. I was told that there was no point in finishing school because it was obvious that I was going to fail everything. I was advised to leave and given the option of being a secretary, a nurse, or an 'air hostess' – those were my career choices when I was sixteen. Luckily, I learned how to type, because several years later this led to my first professional bass job.

A period would go by before Sara would revisit her love of music in any practical way; indeed, it was not until she was based in Leeds, where she was dating a guitar player whose sister was putting a band together, that her interest was piqued and her passion for playing rekindled. Thus, at the age of twenty-one, Sara would purchase her first bass guitar, figuring it couldn't be much different from the classical version she played in the orchestras years ago. 'I had not played for a few years', she admits,

> but I felt like I could take up the bass guitar because I had previously played upright bass, it had the same four strings and fingering. The volume aspect of it was so exciting. Luckily his sister was putting a band together and asked me to play, so I started practising along with records, I had to learn how to play music without having any music to read. That was how it all began.

Sara joined her boyfriend's sister's band as the bass player, which engendered several years of playing in local acts before a fortuitous move to London brought her into contact with the right people to recognize her talent. Once ensconced in the capital, Sara sought employment as a secretary in the Oxford Street offices of Polydor Records, home to The Who, The Jam, and Slade. Now twenty-three and playing the London club circuit whilst holding down the day job, Sara's dynamic rhythmic style grabbed the attention of a notable audience member one fateful night at Camden club The Music Machine. Sara says,

> That's where the typing came in handy! I made friends with the A&R guy at Polydor, so when my band was playing at The Music Machine, I asked him to come to see us because we really wanted a record deal. He said, 'oh, I'm going to that gig anyway because I'm taking somebody to see the opening band'. So, he said he would see me there. About a week later I got a phone call at home from a guy who started telling me how much he enjoyed my playing that

night at The Music Machine and that he particularly enjoyed the chemistry I had with our drummer. When I asked, 'who is this?' he said, 'oh, this is Robert Fripp'. Needless to say, I was somewhat taken aback, he was an artist on Polydor records, I'd seen his record covers hanging on the walls and of course I knew the music of King Crimson.

Fripp invited Sara and the drummer Jonny Toobad to a rehearsal studio to take part in his new art rock project, The League of Gentlemen. Upon arrival she would find one of her musical heroes, Barry Andrews of XTC, awaiting to play alongside her. Sara recalls,

> That was actually a funny coincidence, because as a secretary I of course went to the pub after work with my fellow secretaries and one day I walked into the pub and there was Barry. I loved his band Shriekback, so I put my number on a piece of paper, got up the courage to go over to him and said, 'I'm a bass player, and if you ever need a bass player, I'd love to play with you'. Of course, I never heard from Barry, but six months later I was in a rehearsal studio with him and Robert Fripp. That is how I ended up with League of Gentlemen, because I was a secretary, luckily in the right place at the right time. We rehearsed in a freezing old farmhouse in Dorset, that's where we started making music. It might start with Robert playing a riff, or I would come up with a bassline; likewise, Barry would play something on the keyboards, Jonny would play a groove, and those ideas were developed into the compositions. But the lion's share of the music was written by Robert. He was very fair about it all, he said, 'I want you to go home and figure out what percentage of each song you deserve'... this was all new to me! I'm sure all the music that I played and was exposed to in my child-hood came into play because knowing harmony and the ability to pitch was helpful in that situation; I have good pitch, so I was able to pick things up very quickly. So, I don't doubt that my classical musical background helped when it came to League of Gentlemen. We toured for six months before recording the album, which was a good thing because we had the music down by the time we got to the studio. It was a good way of doing it.

As The League of Gentlemen came to an end, leaving fans of the group with only a tantalizing taste of what could have been before Fripp re-formed King Crimson, Sara received a phone call seeking her presence at Advision Studios in London to record bass for The Soft Boys' frontman Robyn Hitchcock's sophomore album, *Groovy Decay*. While critical approval and commercial appeal eluded the songwriter in his native England throughout this period, the embrace of his Stateside fanbase was more tangibly felt, as Sara would find out in a most unlikely of settings.

> I was in a public toilet in Boston one day and this woman came in and said to me, 'are you Sara Lee?' I said I was, and she proceeded to tell me how much she loved this particular bassline of mine on one of the songs on *Groovy Decay*, which also happened to be my favourite bassline on the record too. So, it was very nice that she came in and said that; it was good to know the music that I had just done with Robyn was out there and reaching people. I love Robyn's songs and really enjoyed playing on that record. It was funny because I had only been playing bass guitar for roughly four years when all this started happening. I didn't know anything about making records, how they were produced, or how one might get a job playing on one, but I got the call to do it and it was an amazing experience.

It was around the autumn of 1981 when Sara would begin her association with Gang of Four. The Leeds band made a significant contribution to the British punk canon with their debut album *Entertainment!* in 1979, and which they followed with *Solid Gold* two years later. The band defined their spare, fiercely rhythmic, and often avant-garde sound on these two seminal releases, amassing great critical respect along the way. Indeed, as punk was threatening to become a caricature of itself, Gang of Four brought sober working-class credibility and street-smart intelligence to their political rhetoric. Whilst grounded in the musical context of punk, the band incorporated generic elements of dub, reggae, and funk, but their rhythmic foundation was disrupted by the departure of bassist Dave Allen, who would leave to play in Shriekback with Sara's former League of Gentlemen bandmate, Barry Andrews. It was when visiting Andrews in the studio that Sara met Allen, who duly informed her that his old gang were looking for her to fill his considerable boots. Allen suggested she call them immediately, and in her doing so Gang of Four would get to work on their third album with a new bassist in tow. The recording of the band's third album, *Songs of the Free*, would resume in Ridge Farm Studios in Surrey, and it was there that Sara's presence would help the band refine a more polished sound that would mark this and their fourth album, *Hard*. While critics were divided and fans lamented the loss of the raw and more esoteric compositions of the first two records, there is no denying the greater sense of melody and groovier rhythms that Sara's presence brought to the band's sonic palette. It was during Sara's three years with Gang of Four that they produced some of their most melodic material, as exemplified with the likes of 'I Love a Man in a Uniform', 'Is It Love', and 'I Fled'. And while these songs may have brought more feet onto the dancefloors of alternative nightclubs throughout the land, Jon King's lyrics remained resolutely political, staunchly satirical and scathing. It was when the slick engineering of those records was stripped away in the live setting that the band proved as powerful as ever, as Sara recalls: 'They were a tremendously powerful band live, more so than on record. Each member of the band brought such a unique presence and style of playing, and Jon's persona onstage is like a man truly possessed. It all added up to them being a truly powerful package in concert'. And as the singles from those albums received greater airplay, the venues being booked reflected the increase in audience. 'We had become very popular in America', Sara confirms, 'the band worked a lot. We were playing to more people in bigger venues than in any other country. The first show I played with them in New York was at the Roseland Ballroom and there was about three thousand or four thousand people in attendance. I don't remember ever playing to that many people in Europe'.

It was whilst touring the East Coast that Sara found an environment in which she could cultivate a career performing with many other artists, and which would keep her active until Gang of Four were to come calling again three decades later. Not knowing if she would ever make it back to New York City if she returned to England with her bandmates after their farewell tour, Sara decided to stick around for a few weeks to catch up with some friends. Those few weeks in 1984 would turn into months, years, and ultimately, decades, as she recalls:

> I loved the music scene, so many clubs and bands and so much easier to get around than in London! I had made some friends over the years who were musicians in New York City and at the end of the farewell tour I decided to stay on for a few weeks because the band had broken up and I didn't know if I would ever come back. People started asking me to play, small gigs here and there, with musicians from the likes of Television and the Patti Smith band, I had landed in that group of downtown NYC musicians, and it was very exciting and eye-opening. Then I met the great drummer Jerry Marotta who took me to see the Neville Brothers and The Meters, I was just blown away. Also, while I was there I got an offer of an audition with Louise Goffin, she was working with a band in LA which was being managed by the Copeland brothers, Miles and Ian, who had been involved with Gang of Four as well. Before we flew to LA, she told me she wanted me to meet two 'phenomenal' drummers in NYC, Charley Drayton and Steve Jordan. We did some playing together and had a great time, but then Louise and I were off for my audition with the band in LA. Someone wanted to make a TV show about a girl band, and they wanted to hire musicians who could actually play as opposed to act. So, I arrive, coming from Gang of Four, black clothes, spiky punk hair and meet the band, all of whom seemed very tall, with long flowing hair and

wearing full body spandex leopard-skin outfits with spiky heels. I thought, this is so LA, this is not me at all, there's no way I can do this! So, Louise and I went back to New York and formed a band with Charley and Steve, Raging Hormones, and it was a great experience for me, a bass player could not ask for a better drummer, and there were two of them! This all happened just four years into being a professional musician, it all felt so different from England and I decided I needed to move to New York. For the next couple of years, I continued playing with Raging Hormones and many others in New York City, I often did two gigs a week at CBGB's with different bands, apart from all the other clubs. Hilly Kristal joked that he would put a bed for me in the back dressing room because I was there so often.

With her financial support nearing depletion, Sara took a job waitressing to make ends meet, determined to stay in the city and find a more sustainable musical solution by becoming part of a band rather than enduring short-term work as a side musician. Soon enough, she would trade carrying plates of food to carrying the grooves of a pop act who were on a steep commercial decline but who had a new album to promote and touring commitments to fulfil. In 1987 Sara received a call from Ireland and it was the Thompson Twins on the line; they wanted Sara to tour with them in support of their new album *Close to the Bone*. That album was the product of the Twins uniting with producer Rupert Hine, and the result was a slick adult-oriented pop record which belied the group's earlier tendencies toward quirky post-punk. As radio friendly as it was, the album may have proved too smooth and bland for their audience who had come of age to their new wave hits 'Doctor! Doctor!' and 'Hold Me Now'. But regardless of the group's popularity, waning or otherwise, being hired for a major tour was a brief respite from the grind of menial work that Sara had found herself mired in. 'I had served enough lunches', she says, 'so when I got the call from the Thompson Twins, I was ready to go. They only had one tour booked, so I was just with them for six months. Being that this was 1987 and in support of the *Close to the Bone* album, it meant that unfortunately the band had peaked beforehand. But it was great fun to play with them'.

After her sojourn on the road with the Thompson Twins, Sara soon found the kind of position she was seeking, a band with whom she would record and tour in the long-term. That band was The B-52s. Sara would join them at a crucial turning point in their career, a moment in which they arose out of tragedy to emerge triumphantly with the greatest success of their career. Just around the corner was the release of the album *Cosmic Thing*, from which the era-defining singles 'Love Shack' and 'Roam' were to be unleashed upon an unsuspecting music world seeking something fun and irreverent to take us out of the social and economic gloom of late 1980s conservative America. It is no wonder that the videos from that album received such heavy rotation; here was a band that brought with them much colour, fun, inclusiveness and diversity, with an aesthetic that drew on left-field and low-brow elements like surf music, sci-fi movies, and 1950s kitsch. To see all of that suddenly become something mainstream was a great moment for late 1980s pop culture, and Sara was right there when it happened, thanks to a downtown acquaintance. Sara recalls,

> I knew a sound guy from CBGB's who had worked with The B-52s and he recommended me to them. They were making their first record since the death of Ricky [guitarist]. They asked me to go on the road and I said yes. They were fun to work with and excited to be playing again after having a two-year break following the tragic loss of Ricky which had impacted them so much. They asked me about a drummer, so I suggested Charley Drayton. I loved playing with him, and I knew it would sound good. Charley didn't want to tour so we auditioned drummers and this time I recommended Zack Alford. I had seen him play a lot when his band played on the same bill as Raging Hormones, every Friday night in a Chinese restaurant behind Port Authority bus station! Zack is a brilliant drummer and moved ahead swiftly after that tour, playing with Bruce Springsteen, David Bowie and Billy Joel. He went from play-ing little clubs in New York with his own band, to working with The B-52s, and then playing with three major artists.

The Love Shack tour proved to be a major turning point for The B-52s, see-ing them go from beloved cult club band to arena superstars over the course of a few months. But with great success came greater responsibilities on the commercial front. The promotional machine proved an intense one, and it was during this major moment for the band that changes were implemented in the line-up. One-third of the frontpeople, Cindy Wilson, took time off from the band for personal reasons and was replaced by Julee Cruise, whose unique, ethereal vocal style had elevated the soundtracks of David Lynch's *Blue Velvet* and *Twin Peaks*. Sara affirms,

> The tour was so much fun, because we started it by playing the likes of CGBG's and Toad's Place in New Haven, all these little clubs, but then four months later we were playing huge venues to 20,000 people a night. It was a terrific rise. They were so unique, nobody had ever heard a band like this before, you could dance to it, the sense of humour, it all made a lot of people happy. But there was also a lot of hard work involved in doing that tour as well, especially for the principles in the band, because of all the stuff that happens

outside of the shows – the promotion and everything that goes with becoming successful. It was a phenomenal amount of work.

And while Sara would go on to record several songs on the band's follow-up record, *Good Stuff*, which was the first B-52s album without Cindy, she was busy working with the next act that would keep her active for much of the 1990s, the Indigo Girls.

'Talk about a full-time job!' Sara exclaims, 'I did a lot with the Indigo Girls, about five records from when I started working with them in 1991 until I left at the end of 1997'. Sara began working with the Atlanta duo on *Nomads Indians Saints*, their second album and one that was released at a time when female-led alternative folk was on trend thanks to successful acts like 10,000 Maniacs and Suzanne Vega. While the Indigo Girls' first album was a stripped-back acoustic affair, *Nomads Indians Saints* called for a fuller production sound which required some skilled studio musicians to flesh it all out for the radio and MTV rotation that was imminent. Sara continues,

> They had done the first record without a bass player, but for *Nomads* they hired me to play bass and Kenny Aronoff to play drums; they brought in a host of other session people too. After I made that record, I didn't see them again for a while until one night when they played in New York. I called them before the show to say that I was coming to see them play and they said, 'Oh, why don't you bring your bass and play a couple of songs with us'. I was in the city, and I had no instruments there, they were back in my place in Woodstock, but I managed to borrow a bass from somebody and spent all afternoon furiously trying to remember how to play these songs that I'd made on the record. So, I went and played with them that night at The Beacon and after the show they asked me if I would like to get on the tour bus and go out on the road. I immediately said, 'Okay!' and I went home, packed a suitcase, and left for six months. That was the beginning of a lot of work with them. They would make a record and three months later you leave to go on the road for ten months, and then start all over again, make another record, tour, etc. We did that cycle for five years, but they took 1996 off. I was very nervous about that, I thought that I might not get another job because I had been with them for so long, but then Ani [DiFranco] called me out of the blue and asked me if I was available. I ended up playing with Ani for that year, it was tremendous fun, she's a powerhouse and with that trio we rocked the halls around America. I went back to the Indigo Girls for one more year and then I left. I knew it was time for me to do some other music. And then ironically The B-52s called and asked me to go back to them. I did a few more years with them doing mostly corporate gigs

and very limited touring during the summers. Sterling Campbell, who had previously played with David Bowie and Duran Duran, was their drummer at this point. It wasn't a lot of work with The B-52s in those years but it was certainly consistent work, something like two corporate shows a month.

With the passage of time and almost twenty years of performing on other artists' records and tours, Sara felt the pull of the muse to write and release her own solo album. But for someone who enjoyed the relative anonymity of being a side musician, the idea of becoming the face and voice of a project was more than a little daunting. 'I was going to become forty-five-years old in 2000', Sara recalls, 'I didn't want to get to the age of fifty and say, "why didn't I ever make my own record?" I thought I should try; I'd never written songs before, just dabbled around with some musical ideas on my 8-track or my 4-track, whatever it was we had in those days!'

And try she did. However, some assistance was required as Sara was neither a songwriter nor lyricist, though she was not short of musical ideas that proved successful as seeds of songs to come. 'I felt like I really needed some help with structuring my ideas', she reveals, 'so my manager introduced me to songwriter Maggie Ryder, and we started writing some music together. I had several writers contribute lyrics, Emily [Saliers], Ani and my friends Barbara Gogan, the lead singer with The Passions, and Pal Shazar'. After writing several songs with Ryder, Sara felt confident enough to move forward and endeavour to write songs on her own. But being a frontperson would be a whole new world for the erstwhile side player; it was a position she had never envisioned for herself, having never sought the centre stage spotlight. While she loved being the bass player in the back, laying down the groove and keeping the rhythm right, she emerged from the wings for her solo sojourn with the wonderfully eclectic album *Make it Beautiful*, a record resplendent in soul, funk, and R&B. Sonically rich, it was mixed by Grammy Award-winning producer-engineer Neil Dorfsman, whose work can be heard on some of the best-sounding records of the 1980s, including Bruce Hornsby and the Range's *Scenes from the Southside*, Dire Straits' *Money for Nothing*, and Carly Simon's *Coming Around Again*. Sara says,

> My manager was friends with Neil, so he mixed it and he was amazing, and we recorded it at the great Bearsville Studios. Even though I don't play guitar I wrote some specific guitar parts, and it is times like that where the classical training came in handy because it meant I could write something out in musical notation for another instrument even though I wasn't any good at playing the instrument itself. To record the guitar, I hired a guy called Adam Widoff, who is hands down one of my absolute favourite guitar players in the whole world. And I knew so many great drummers that I had

some of them play on the album – Zack Alford, Charley Drayton, and Carla Azar, who played with Wendy and Lisa. It was an amazing feeling to have written music, to hear it come to fruition and actually be in a recording studio, getting it down on 2-inch tape! My producer Peter Scherer worked with me tirelessly, and towards the end I was so fortunate to have Neil Dorfsman come in to mix it. It was just fabulous to hear my music coming out of those Bearsville Studio speakers.

Make it Beautiful would be released on Ani DiFranco's label Righteous Babe Records in 2000, and while Sara found the experience of making the record to be an incredibly rewarding artistic experience, she would have to come to terms with the responsibilities of being a frontwoman and embrace the fact that she was now the face of the music.

Being a side person, I was able to work with many different artists, it was musically interesting, challenging and enjoyable, at least most times! Sometimes I was given songs to learn in advance, other times I heard them for the first time when I turned up to work in the recording studio. On the best days, I heard a song for the first time and the bass line just seemed to immediately flow out of me, an example of that happening is 'Galileo' by the Indigo Girls. Although of course, in that particular case, it never hurts to have a drummer of the calibre of Jerry Marotta to play along with. In the 'good old days' we used to spend a day on each song with the full band getting the backing tracks, it was so much fun. After the demise of big recording budgets artists often weren't able to hire a full band, so it was common to be recording alone to pre-recorded tracks and working much more quickly, I remember making at least one full album in a day. One other benefit of being a side person is that occasionally you have an unexpected opportunity for a magnificent moment. For me, one of these was when Emily asked me to score a string arrangement for her song 'Caramia'. It was in 6/8 and quite a rhythmic part. As good fortune would have it, the Atlanta Symphony orchestra was on strike when we were recording, so eleven of the string players came to the studio for the session and due to the prevailing circumstances, I actually ended up conducting. What a thrilling experience that was, one of the absolute highlights of my musical career.

According to Sara,

Doing shows as a frontperson was of course completely new, it was something I'd never planned on being. I didn't quite know how I would be able to pull it off. I love playing bass, being in the background, holding it down with the drums, I never wanted to be the main focus of attention. But I was quite surprised how easily I slipped into it actually, it didn't feel as difficult as I thought it would be, to sing lead vocal while playing bass and at times simultaneously playing my Moog bass pedals as well! It was a whole lot of fun. When it came to going out on the road, I needed a drummer who wasn't one of those people on the album and that is because I had no money, but luckily, I met a phenomenal drummer in Woodstock named Joe Magistro and he came on the road with me. For the live guitar I brought in my dear friend Ann Klein, who is a fantastic guitar player. Then it came time for our first gig, which was opening for Ani DiFranco. I wish there had been more time for me to practise being a lead singer before opening for Ani DiFranco. It was trial by fire!

Taking the album out on the road would prove to be a whole other beast to conquer thanks to the cultural changes that were occurring in the music business at the time. This was the moment that ushered in unlimited digital access to commercial art such as film, music, and literature. These industries saw their product devalued in the eyes of the consumer, who no longer felt the need to pay premium prices for physical product. Sara says,

> I would get people coming up to me at these shows where I was getting paid a hundred bucks and they would say, 'oh, we heard your record, we downloaded it from Napster'. I felt, 'okay, how am I supposed to make a living?' There was no way that I could afford to tour, and I wasn't making enough money from selling records. I opened for K.D. Lang and for some other people, but I couldn't sustain it. I won't say what each person was paying me, but I will say that I was getting paid anywhere between $100 a night to $500 a night, playing at places like The Beacon Theatre in New York. I knew $500 was the standard for that kind of band as an opener, so that was fine because you can sort of make that work. But being a side person myself, I was not going to ask my musicians to do it for nothing; that is something you get asked a lot, you're always told 'we haven't got any money!' but I wanted to pay my musicians a hundred bucks a night. I also had other expenses, such as having to rent the van and get two hotel or motel rooms. I was constantly putting my own money into this band, and I was going to end up going through all my savings if I kept it up, so I just couldn't afford to do it anymore. And then I thought that there was no point doing any more records because I couldn't afford to promote them.

Sara continued to plug, and play, *Make it Beautiful* for a year, occasionally going back to The B-52s for corporate concerts, and throughout the next decade she would continue collaborating with the likes of Natalie Merchant and Satellite Paradiso, the latter a project of The Psychedelic Furs' founding guitarist and her former Woodstock neighbour, John Ashton. Then in 2009 Sara would be called upon for a series of shows filling in for bassist Rachel Haden on Todd Rundgren's Arena tour. 'I've had many memorable experiences in my career but that was one of the true standout moments for me', she exclaims.

> That was an incredible project and how it came about was Todd had been out on the road for a year-long tour, but his bass player couldn't do the last five shows and, somehow, I was recommended to him. I was only there for about a week, but what a time it was, and what a talent Todd is. He was so entertaining to be with, hanging out at the airport and chatting with him was always fun; he is a very friendly, enjoyable person to be around. And the band was amazing; Prairie Prince was the drummer, the guitar player was Jesse Gress, and they have been with Todd for decades. Todd goes through these evolving musical phases wherein he makes completely different sounding records, a bit like David Bowie did, and the record he was promoting on this tour was called *Arena*, so the music was very much 'arena rock'. That kind of music was a million miles from anything I had done in my life or ever wanted to do, I never thought about doing music like that at all. But, oh my god, it was so enjoyable to be playing these full-on, blasting rock songs with musicians who were so adept at playing that kind of stuff; they are such accomplished musicians they could play anything. I wish that had been a longer tour, I would have given anything to play with Todd for longer.

In the interim, touring took a backseat in Sara's life. The practicalities of life on the road took their toll. 'I couldn't tour anymore', she discloses.

> I was utterly burnt out, so I kind of removed myself from it for the last fifteen years. I just wanted to stay home. I never had a successful relationship, and then I met the person that I wanted to be with. I played the odd gig locally and did some little recordings, getting to play with some great people in the process, but I had toured for twenty-seven years, and I was just done with it. My experience of being on the road is not great; I love playing shows, but I can't sleep on the bus and I'm just tired of driving around all these places which look the same. It's almost depressing to think about it because so much about touring America is repetition. You end up

seeing the same old staples such as Walmart and so many places which lack character. Touring Europe is so interesting. The towns are hundreds of years old, each with their own character, but in many places that we hit in the US I felt, 'is there anything different around here?' I don't mean to sound like a European snob because there are many fantastic places in America, but that's all part of being a working musician. Sometimes a job comes your way, and you have a blast, and then other jobs come along and it's like, 'oh well, I've got to pay the rent!' and you get on the bus.

However, one of those jobs which fits firmly into the former came along in 2022, with her touring career coming full circle when the reformed Gang of Four sought Sara out for bass duties once again, thirty years since first joining the Leeds group.

The recent Gang of Four thing was a complete surprise, I didn't know how it would work in terms of me enjoying being out on the road again. They said to me that they were going to go out for a few weeks with the view to possibly doing more. I told them that I would agree to do the initial few weeks, I committed to doing that, saying, 'if I can cope with life on the road and it goes well, I'll do more'. Then when we did go out on tour, we had an incredible time. Working with them again now there are things that I noticed that I didn't notice the first time I joined the band. That is partly because back then I was young and having fun on the road and not paying attention. You didn't see so many videos of live performances of yourself back then, whereas now you see them all the time. I've been able to understand things like the extent of Jon's ability and capacity as a performer. He is an incredible frontperson. Another thing that has been reinforced to me when working with them recently is how unique a drummer Hugo is. Of course, Andy was a truly original guitar player, nobody plays guitar like that, but it is important to note that the new guitar player, David Pajo, who has replaced Andy, is phenomenal. When I arrived at the studio on the first day of rehearsal it didn't take long before we were enjoying being in each other's company again. I hadn't seen Jon for decades, I had seen Hugo maybe three times since 1984, but we were immediately cracking each other up. And in the middle of the room is this poor man who is 'the new guy'. He was apparently a fan of ours, a big fan of Andy Gill's, and he's there to fill Andy's shoes! So, we said we better stop joking around and start rehearsing, and when this guy began playing my jaw could have dropped to the floor. It was incredible, he sounded exactly like Andy, and it wasn't just the notes he played, because Andy didn't just play notes, it was noises and feedback and scratches, all these different sounds, but David got everything precisely right. And then as the hours went by, he brought more of his own playing into it. It was very exciting to find him and have him playing with us, we really couldn't have got a better replacement. It was hard to imagine how we were going to get someone who could do the same thing as Andy, but he really worked out great. So, we're at a point now where we are all excited to do more touring and where I look forward to working with them again. Looking back on my career, I realize I've been blessed to have worked with so many fantastic musicians, having shared so many great times in the studio and on the road with them.

7 Lori Barbero

It didn't take long for anyone who was firmly entrenched in the Minneapolis alternative music community of the mid-1980s to take notice of a vibrant young woman who worked in local clubs and frequented the many shows that marked the Twin Cities as ground zero for Midwestern alt-rock. Lori Barbero was impossible to ignore. A fierce champion of local and national acts who rolled through town, she was an omnipresent figure within the thriving club scenes of the city. But within a few years Lori herself would become a major part of the alternative music explosion of the early 1990s as the drummer for her seminal rock band, Babes in Toyland. She toured the world sharing stages with Rage Against the Machine and the Beastie Boys; one could turn on MTV and there she was hosting *120 Minutes*, not to mention being featured along-side Nirvana and Sonic Youth in the big screen documentary *1991: The Year Punk Broke*. But before that Lori was this ubiquitous figure on the Minneapolis music scene. She had her own record label, managed artists, and booked tours. Every band that came to town stayed at Lori's house, no doubt enjoying her skate ramp and other hospitalities; she was heavily involved in every aspect of the underground music community. But as definitive a Minnesotan as Lori is, she spent her formative years growing up in Rockland County, a suburb of New York City, moving there when her father was transferred to work in a city bank. Lori would attend Pearl River High School from ninth to twelfth grades, all the while feeling the lure of the musical metropolis that she could view from her bedroom window. Lori says,

> There wasn't much of a music culture in my family, but we did have one of those huge console stereos that had these giant speakers, a record player, and an FM radio in it. There was always music on all day every day, stuff like The Fifth Dimension, Herb Alpert and the Tijuana Brass Band, and Sergio Mendes, all that kind of stuff. So, I was just listening to music all the time. My grandmother on my

father's side liked all the old blues and soul, which is what I listen to also, so it always triggers something when I hear it. But I didn't know much about it back then, I was just taking it all in. But then I started going into the city and I saw all the bands, so I became really involved in music there, it was a big part of my life. I would go into the city to see Queen, David Bowie, Patti Smith, The Dead Boys, and Television. So, music really started for me when I was in high school in the mid-'70s.

After high school Lori went to QS Florida University whilst living on a houseboat and working at Sloppy Joe's to make ends meet. But soon enough she moved to what would become her spiritual hometown and truly immersed herself in the burgeoning Minneapolis music scene. Once there she took work at bustling music clubs such as the punk-rock bar The Long Horn, and a downtown venue called The Uptown. The latter was the spawning ground of all those fantastic Twin Cities bands that would soon become revered as alternative acts, some of whom would morph into mainstream rock bands: Husker Du, Soul Asylum, and The Replacements. It was there at The Uptown that one could see The Jayhawks when they were just starting out or Run Westy Run for a dollar on a Friday night. Bands became national or international from that spot. Lori affirms,

> Our music scene was so vibrant, it was just a plethora of bands playing seven nights a week. I miss The Uptown more than anything else in the Twin Cities. [Replacements bassist] Tommy Stinson's mom, Anita, worked there as the bartender for thirtysomething years. The place rarely had a cover charge, and if they did it was maybe $3 to see Nirvana, but it was super, super fun having live music every night of the week. And five of those seven nights were shows by touring bands, not local, so I got exposed to a lot of music that I wouldn't have otherwise experienced. It was a real musical education for me and everyone who worked there got to know the bands. Some of them came by to play there so early in their careers, whether it was Afghan Whigs, The Flaming Lips, or Nirvana, and they wouldn't even have their own sound engineer, they would just use our house guys.

Minnesota harboured a true music community and while The Uptown was the breeding ground for much talent, another mecca for local artists and fans was First Avenue, a former disco club turned landmark concert venue after being made famous by Prince upon recording his signature song 'Purple Rain' there in August 1983. First Avenue was also notable as a musician's preferred place to perform because the sound was so incredible. They really got it right there. Even for the audience, the sound was good no matter where you were standing in the club. But this was too big of a venue for many of the smaller alternative acts who were still building their following, as First Avenue hosted predominantly larger international bands playing to audiences of a thousand or more. However, the tiny sidebar attached to it called 7th St. Entry, with its capacity of 250, provided yet another stage for emerging alt-rockers, local and national, and where Husker Du recorded their legendary live album, *Land Speed Record*. Lori says,

> You had to have a huge following to play First Avenue, the smaller bands certainly didn't play there, but they played 7th St. Entry once it opened, so between there and The Uptown I was out seven nights a week seeing all this happening. It was an amazing time. It's hard to get rock bands to play in town now because there just aren't any musicians around anymore, it's all computers and tech oriented. There's not much that blows my skirt up anymore.

In 1986, Lori made a purchase that would help her become an even more intrinsic part of the scene that she helped support so rigorously. While managing Run Westy Run, Lori was spurred on by their friend Jim Harry to invest in her first drumkit, knowing her fascination with the instrument, or perhaps knowing her fascination with those who played it. 'When I went to shows it was always the drummer that left me with my mouth open', Lori admits.

> I became a heavy-duty mouth-breather because my jaw would just drop watching the drummer because there was something captivating about watching all four limbs do four different things at once. It was like watching this human machine, it just made me hot and horny, even though I never knew or found out any of their names, I just knew I was infatuated with them. I had no idea what the individual drums were called, I didn't know what a hi-hat was or what a ride cymbal was, or a bass drum or a floor tom, I was just like 'The Drummers!'

However, Lori's new acquisition would sit untouched in her closet until, at the age of twenty-seven, she met a young guitar player called Kat Bjelland, and the rest is music, and Minneapolis, history. She says,

> Most people are ready to retire from music at twenty-seven, and I didn't know what I was going to do with my drumkit until I met Kat in 1987. I saw her around the city a lot, at shows and at afterparties, so we just started hanging out and practising in my basement. She would play guitar and I would play drums along with her and before long we had whole songs where I would be just playing the same beat over and over again. I have old recordings on cassette

of us playing and you can clearly hear that when we were done with each song we would boisterously start laughing because it was so fucking hysterical to us that we could do it. That was the start of Babes in Toyland.

With a punk-rock DIY resolve to not let a lack of practical or theoretical musical education get in her way, Lori drew upon the influence of some drummer friends for guidance and inspiration, including Grant Hart of Husker Du. Lori says,

> I was self-taught, but I would watch Grant play and I had a boyfriend who was the drummer in a Twin Cities band called Man Sized Action and I learned a lot from watching him. I was subconsciously lifting things from these guys. Another influence on my playing was Public Image Ltd. I was listening to their album *Flowers of Romance* recently and I realised just how much I totally scammed that tribal style of drumming from it. I really didn't mean to rip them off, but it was just deep down in me. I'm a tom-tom girl! That's where I started and that's where I remain.

Musical chops be damned, but raw power all the way, it didn't take long for Babes in Toyland to become an integral part of the Minneapolis music scene and build up a core fanbase that would elevate them to the next phase of their career: signing a record deal. The band inked a contract with Twin/Tone Records, home of The Replacements, Husker Du, Soul Asylum, Ween, Robyn Hitchcock, and to whom Information Society was once signed. Lori says,

> We got with Twin/Tone because we were local and no one could ignore us, we were just so loud and raunchy... and we were women! So, it all happened very quickly for us. We signed the record deal, and we were out touring pretty soon as well. Dan Kaminsky was a good friend of mine who was in a band from Milwaukee and when they were going on tour he asked if we would be the first band to open for them. The other band on the tour was White Zombie. That was literally eight or nine months after the first time Kat and I got together.

The debut Babes in Toyland album, *Spanking Machine*, was laid down at Reciprocal Recording in Seattle in 1989 and released the following year. It is as raw as any underground '80s LA punk LP or any New York hardcore record, defying what some critics may call 'the Minneapolis sound' when referring to other major acts that emerged from the scene. But then Babes in Toyland defied all trends in forging their own path and influencing other acts and movements to come. 'There was an LA hardcore band called Legal Weapon who had a singer named Kat Arthur and they blew me away', Lori recalls.

> I remember thinking if I'm ever going to be in a band, I want to sound this hardcore and this awesome. But when it came to developing our own sound, Babes in Toyland didn't want to be like anybody else. Kat just played guitar in this really great way which was distinctly hers, and I learned to drum by playing alongside her and doing it in my own style, so we got our own thing going and that was our sound. Some people don't like her vocal style because she screams, but she is just an unbelievable singer-songwriter-guitarist.

By now Babes in Toyland were confirmed local heroes on the Minneapolis music scene, but they were also picking up crucial national momentum through touring and hard work in building a massive fan base. Indicative of the booming alternative music culture that was rising fast into mainstream culture, Lori and her bandmates signed a multiple-album record deal with Warner/Reprise. Babes in Toyland they may have been, but they were no babes in the woods, as they insisted upon maintaining their artistic integrity despite the commercial implications of signing with a major label. Thankfully for them, they had just the right people in their corner when it came to negotiating contracts and navigating this new corporate musical landscape, as Lori recalls:

> Richard Grabel, who was Madonna's and Sonic Youth's lawyer, represented us and the one thing we wanted on our contract was one hundred per cent creative freedom and he made sure we got that. There was one time when our manager tried to tell us that we needed to do this and do that, and we had to bring certain bands on tour because it would really help us, and we were like 'screw you…Screw! You!' Fortunately for us our A&R guy was Tim Carr, but he was really the fourth member of our band. He was the greatest man on the planet. I miss him horribly. If anyone knew Tim Carr was on our side, they wouldn't even try mess with us. He was respected. So, it was a win-win situation for us. And it is because of him that we crossed paths with so many great people like Vito Acconci, Arto Lindsay, and Cindy Sherman, who did our record cover and would be Kat's doppelgänger in one of our videos. He introduced us to Diamanda Galás, who would come and hang out at our shows, and we got to know Megadeth and the Beastie Boys. We would go to parties at Mike D's house with his big pool out in LA. Without Tim Carr none of that would ever have happened.

After signing their major label deal and assuming the autonomy they so desired, what happened next for Babes in Toyland was a whirlwind of international touring, performing at major American festivals, taking over MTV, and making enough noise to leave a lasting impression on the male-dominated rock scene. The sound and influence of Minneapolis bands like Husker Du and The Replacements can be heard in many of the Seattle bands that emerged in the early 1990s, and filmmaker Cameron Crowe essentially highlighted that connection when he hired lead Replacement Paul Westerberg to write the music for his grunge scene movie, *Singles*, in 1991. The film and its subsequent soundtrack album places Westerberg alongside the likes of Seattle scenesters Alice in Chains, Mother Love Bone, Pearl Jam, and the Screaming Trees, and in doing so it is easy to trace the sonic lineage of 'the Minneapolis sound' to that of 'the Seattle sound'. Further establishing the musical DNA between the scenes was Dave Markey's documentary *1991: The Year Punk Broke*, which featured Babes in Toyland alongside Seattle acts Nirvana and Mudhoney. Something important and seminal occurred in the underground Minneapolis music scene that went national, engendering a moment when those local heroes became critically adored and commercially successful acts for corporate record companies; so, it was perhaps inevitable that these artists would influence the emerging movements to come, such as grunge. Those connections are inextricably drawn with the likes of Crowe's and Markey's films placing them side-by-side, as well as with grunge artists name-checking Minneapolis bands as major influences. But Babes in Toyland could hardly be considered a part of the grunge genre, either sonically or aesthetically. To those that came up through punk rock and everything that followed, it all sounds like garage rock. It was the sound of kids who played in their basements, purely and recognizably alternative, no matter what label was put on it by journalists or by the industry to try to conveniently market the band to specific demographic groups. 'Thurston Moore once wrote that we were the "Grandmothers of Grunge"!' Lori says, bemused by the generic tag.

> But we just considered ourselves a girl band who were just as great as any guy band, and we worked ten times harder. And we were never a political band either, though we never let anyone fuck with us. If we come out there and you scream 'show us your tits!' I will come down there and bite your two-inch wiener off! That shit just doesn't fly with us. But that time was just so much fun for us. I couldn't have done anything more that would have made any of it any greater. It felt as though Kat and I had conquered the world because we were the originals in the band, we worked really hard, and we were fortunate to achieve what we did. They really were the best of times. We played the Reading Festival in England, which is documented in the film *The Year That Punk Broke*, and we went out on tour across the country with the likes of My Bloody Valentine,

Faith No More, The Melvins, White Zombie, and then we went all over Europe with Sonic Youth. Another highlight was being on Lollapalooza. We did that in '93 and it was just a blast. We were on the whole tour, going from venue-to-venue with all these other bands who were just blowing up at the time. Primus and Alice in Chains co-headlined and other bands on the bill were Dinosaur Jr., Rage Against the Machine, Arrested Development, and Tool.

Despite the attention of the music media and an increasing presence on the world's stage, Babes in Toyland stayed true to their intentions, as evidenced with their subsequent albums, *Fontanelle* and *Nemesisters* which successfully retain the feral, uncompromising sound of the band. Those albums are as raw and sonically powerful as their debut, avoiding the kind of commercial compromises that so many previously alternative artists succumb to when signing with major labels. Lori and her bandmates also maintained a physical presence in Minneapolis and a crucial connection to their punk-rock roots by recording much of their second and third albums in their hometown and utilizing local talent to assist in the releases. She recalls,

We did occasionally go to other cities, including New York for ses-sions with Lee Ranaldo from Sonic Youth, but we didn't use any of those recordings on the albums. We also recorded stuff in Seattle at Reciprocal Studios with Jack Endino, who recorded all the Sub Pop bands at the time. But spending time in Minneapolis had a lot to do with the influence that bands like Minor Threat and Sonic Youth had on us with their DIY attitude; since day one I learned that you don't have to go far to get what you need, you can support people in your own backyard, and they can support you. So, our photographer, our video director, our makeup artist, everyone, they were all people we found in our own backyard. You don't have to go to LA to find the best person. That's how I was taught by those bands with a DIY ethic, I just watched and listened and learned, and after doing it a couple of times I realized that's the only way I could ever do it. When you know somebody who is a photographer, why not use them? I mean it's ridiculous to have to fly somewhere just to have someone take photos of you, that's the most ridiculous thing in the world.

Just as the band were reaching their pop-cultural peak in the mid-1990s, the alternative music that rocked the world for the past decade was driven either back underground or into the charts, but the happy medium of being an uncompromising yet successful alternative act wasn't sustainable. Babes in Toyland and Warner/Reprise parted ways after two albums, and while the band would continue in various configurations for a couple of years, the band members went their separate ways until their much-celebrated 2015 reunion, which was heralded by none other than their old touring partner, Tom Morello of Rage Against the Machine, who introduced and recounted the importance of the band at their comeback show at The Roxy Theatre in Los Angeles.

'The reunion was great', Lori declares.

> We didn't hang out for a few years and then we got back together. It was serious but we really enjoyed it. We were older, so we were more mature and grounded and when you're grounded you are more focused, when you're younger on tour you're just spun. I didn't think we would be able to do it, but we were almost better than we were before. For the final show of the reunion, we played with the Foo Fighters, Queens of the Stone Age, Bob Mould, and The Kills. The whole thing was a great opportunity to bring all the ladies that we love out with us on the road. We brought Skating Polly to Europe, we brought Kitten Forever across the States, and we had a San Antonio band called Fea, for whom I produced some songs on their album which was released on Joan Jett's Blackheart Records label. Since our earliest headlining days, we used mostly local bands to open for us because I always like to support local artists.

And supporting local artists is what Lori has been doing in the years since the dissolution of Babes in Toyland, though they are now a younger breed of musician than she was in the habit of helping. Lori has been involved in setting up a girls' rock school in St. Paul, Minnesota, a testament to the musician's do-it-yourself ethic and the communal spirit of the alternative scene that Minneapolis will always be celebrated for. Lori says proudly,

> I started an all-girls music studio, and I did it with Chris Larson and Corey Avery. It was a very challenging project which started out as Chris's idea; he had an art studio in which he built a soundproof studio, and he wanted me and Corey to join him. Another woman, Miki Mosman, also got involved as she documented it all. We let the girls name it; they put their ideas into a hat, and we voted on SARG – 'Super Awesome Rocker Girls'. That was the idea of a girl named Monique who was six years old. We let them do everything, we just facilitated it; we had women there every weekend to chaperone and answer any questions the kids might have. Our girls ranged from ages six to sixteen; it was a safe space for them. They were mostly kids from disadvantaged families who couldn't afford expensive guitars, amps, and drum kits, kids with nowhere to go and nothing to do. We didn't teach instruments, they learned it all

themselves, they learned how to play, learned how to be a band, learned how to write songs, and when they were done we recorded them and put out a 7' record, something they'll have thirty years from now. They did the artwork for the record, for the posters, and the t-shirts. They named the songs; they named the band. It was all about these young girls making 100% creative choices. Like what we did in Babes in Toyland.

8 Caroline Dale

Caroline Dale's credits read like a who's who of rock'n'roll royalty – appearances on tours and albums with U2, Page and Plant, Oasis, David Gilmour, and many others of their ilk. But Caroline's was not the typical route one takes to make it onstage with such major rock acts; her musical awakening did not occur in spit-stained SoHo clubs like the Roxy or the Vortex. No, for Caroline, the world of music opened for her at the age of five when the Elgar cello concerto came on the radio, performed by one Jacqueline du Pré. The eminent prodigy du Pré would prove to be more than a passing influence in Caroline's life, in fact they would reach a personal connection later, but du Pré's prowess on the cello that day was enough to cement her fascination with the instrument and to declare to her mother, 'that's what I want to do!' Fortunately, Caroline's parents were sympathetic to the study of music; they were both accomplished biologists who in their youth harboured ambitions to play instruments, but time moved on. Caroline says,

> They never had a chance to learn, so they started us all on piano at the age of five. There was my oldest sister Sue and my youngest sister Miranda. None of us were particularly gifted at the piano but Miranda was very good at the violin, which she started on when she was three. She took to it like a duck to water. Out of the three kids, two of us had perfect pitch. However, I never really took to piano, my coordination between my right hand and left hand is really shit. I always loved singing and I would just sing around the house. But just before my sixth birthday I listened to this piece of music on the radio and it turned out to be the Elgar cello concerto with Jacqueline du Pré playing and I said to my mum, 'that's what I want to do and that's what I want to play!' and she said, 'that's all very well, Caroline, but you are very short so I don't think that is going to be possible'. But I begged her and begged her and eventually

persuaded her because there was an old viola knocking around the house that I used to put between my legs and pretend I was playing the cello. So, I eventually got my first lesson. You know when you take to something, and it just feels completely right? As much as I was no good at piano, I was very gifted at learning to play the cello. It just seemed to come really naturally. The piano seems to be very much a left brain–right brain thing and didn't work for me, but the cello did, and I just had so much fun playing it. I never considered 'practising' it, I just picked it up and played it all the time; then I started singing lessons as well. Sue went on to do some artistic things in her own way and eventually became an Assistant Stage Manager for the Royal Shakespeare Company. Sue was the brainy one and found it very difficult to figure out what she wanted to do, but she ended up in the Arts in some way. Miranda and I just really took to playing music. When I was eleven, I took lessons in Middlesbrough, where we all grew up; it was not a very rich and affluent area but at the time there was a very strong Labour council and they all believed that everyone should have a chance at playing an instrument and joining a little orchestra, so a lot of musicians came from Middlesbrough around that time and are still in the profession today. It really shows what good education can do.

When Caroline was eleven years old, and upon the suggestion of her music teacher, she had the good fortune to play before a former professor at the Royal Academy of Music who took note of the young cello enthusiast. Florence Hooton was a noted cellist who had recorded for Decca in the 1930s before bringing her skills to the halls of academia. Impressed with the child's skills, Hooten then recommended that she travel down to London once a month for further tutoring. Hooten would become Caroline's teacher for over a decade.

Florence was a wonderful woman. My teacher had met her on a course somewhere and suggested she listen to me. And she did, so I took lessons with her for twelve years after that. Bless my parents, I don't know how they managed to do that because in those days it was at least a five- or six-hour trip down the motorway to have a one-hour lesson and then drive back. So, it was a chore for my mum and dad for sure, but because of that I won the Young Musician of the Year when I was thirteen and that is what propelled me on to the fast track to my musical career in terms of doing concerts. It was around this time that I went to the Royal Academy of Music, I was let in early into the junior academy, and when I was sixteen it was O-Levels time and they allowed me to do the smallest number of O-Levels to get into the Academy. I shouldn't have gone to the Academy until I was eighteen, but I went when I was sixteen. It was normal that you had to choose piano as a second subject, but I was begging my piano teacher to let me stop because I was so bad at it; I got to Grade 6 and it was just a pain for everyone concerned. I love the piano, don't get me wrong, I was just not very good at it. So, I asked if I could possibly do singing instead. I loved studying singing and that was something I was eventually able to use later on for backing vocals. So, studying cello and singing was a nice combination.

With ambition to burn, Caroline entered the BBC Young Musician of the Year competition, and after coming first in the String finals, the very person who initiated Caroline's immersion into music stepped forward to introduce herself as an admirer. It was Jacqueline du Pré.

She wrote to me after I won that String final and said, 'I just want to meet you and talk about Life, Love, and Cello'. It was an absolute honour to meet her – as being a fourteen-year-old meeting your hero would be – but she had MS quite badly and it was terrible to see her so debilitated, it was such a tragedy. But she used to come along to my concerts. When I'd do a recital in London she would come along in her wheelchair. I wish I had met her younger, but it was fantastic to make that connection. She was my role model because I would consider her a bit of a rock'n'roll cellist in the way that she was very spontaneous; she was natural, for her it came completely from the heart, and it was completely felt. There was a real guts to her playing. You get the feeling that whatever way she woke up that morning dictated the way she was going to play, there was a real instantaneous reaction to the music every day.

At the age of sixteen, Caroline received an opportunity to study her instrument in foreign lands when she won the Julius Isserlis Scholarship, a study-abroad award funded by the Royal Philharmonic Society which took her first to Switzerland, then to Canada. It was in Geneva that she would get to study with her cello hero, Pierre Fournier, the erstwhile 'aristocrat of cellists'.

I won the scholarship, but because I was so young and had only just got to the Academy at the age of sixteen, I had lessons with Pierre, who was an amazing guy. But then the following year I had to use the money abroad, so I literally had to leave, and I left when I was eighteen. If I didn't use the money I would lose it, so my teacher said, 'you've got to go, you have to fly the nest now. So why don't you spend half the time in Geneva with Pierre Fournier and the other half in Banff?' And Banff is this amazing place in Canada, I had an incredible time there. They have a great ethos, certainly for the postgrad – even though I wasn't a postgrad, I was just eighteen! But you had to have a goal, and my particular goal was learning a program and doing a concert back in the UK with it. But it could be any goal at all. But they had this floating faculty, so I could take whatever piece I was learning not necessarily to a cellist but to a flautist or to a pianist, but it was all set in the woods in Banff and it was fantastic. So, I spent quite a few years bopping along and loving that. Then I went home and won another competition called Young Concert Artists Trust, which meant that I would come back and fulfil all these concerts.

I was feeling very rebellious at this stage because I felt like I was pushed into this direction that I didn't particularly want to go. I don't know whether somebody was indeed pushing me or if I was just going along with everything – it was like that feeling of the train being in motion and you can't get off, and that is why I started to diversify. And the first diversification was playing in a Contemporary Dance band. How it really happened was I had spent a lot of time with piano and cello repertoire, and I found it to be quite a lonely existence. I always loved playing with other people and enjoyed other aspects of music like the pop world, but I felt that when I got back from Geneva, where I'd studied, it was quite a rarefied atmosphere; when I'd meet my friends from the Academy, I'd hear they were all doing lovely stuff and one of the things they were doing was touring with London Contemporary Dance. Then my friend Andy said, 'I don't know if you would be interested but the cellist has gone sick, would you be interested in going on a little tour?' I was like, 'Yes! Yes! Absolutely yes!' I just wanted to stop doing what I was doing and go try something completely different. It was my first professional gig where I wasn't just a soloist; I got to be just one of the gang. And I loved touring around, whether it was having a weekend in Portsmouth here or a weekend in Edinburgh there, maybe a few days in Leeds. Wherever it was. Just travelling around. Having spent so long talking to musicians I find that we are kind of like gypsies, touring is the thing that we love.

Touring would indeed become a major component of Caroline's career as a musician, and her much sought-after presence within the live pop and rock world can no doubt be attributed to her notable collaborations with producer John Reynolds, and by extension Sinead O'Connor. Having made an impression on the music world with his work on O'Connor's debut album, *The Lion and the Cobra* (1987), Reynolds would go on to make a name for himself as a drummer, composer, and producer of note with the likes of Jah Wobble, Nan

Vernon, Adam Ant, and Indigo Girls. However, it was O'Connor's success which was crucial for Reynolds's career and for those who would recurrently work for him. O'Connor proved to be the nucleus of a particular team of talent, with her professional and personal association with Reynolds drawing in a close-knit community of musicians who would benefit by working regularly with the pair (who had married in 1987 but later separated). With her 1990 album *I Do Not Want What I Haven't Got*, O'Connor became supernova. A cover of Prince's 'Nothing Compares 2 U' would make her famous, but a controversial appearance on *Saturday Night Live* in 1992 would make her infamous. After singing an a cappella version of Bob Marley's 'War', O'Connor held aloft a photograph of Pope John Paul II and proceeded to tear it to pieces in front of a shocked worldwide audience. Notoriety would plague the singer, and the public's perception of her as a truculent artist didn't necessarily damage her reputation within the musician fraternity. O'Connor faced the challenges of celebrity in a most public manner over the next few years, but her musical integrity was never in doubt. She continued recording albums that defied the expectations of a commercial artist, while putting together exceptional bands for her tours in support of them. The drummer for these tours was usually John Reynolds, who would draw upon his recurring cast of musicians; the de facto musical director, his ensemble would feature the likes of Clare Kenny (she of Indigo Girls, Damien Dempsey, etc., as detailed in an earlier chapter) on bass, and Caroline on cello.

> From the moment I met John I knew I had a friend for life. He has brought things out of me that most people wouldn't be able to. He is just an amazing man. It was another one of those situations where I was incredibly lucky. I had been asked to do Nigel Kennedy's Quartet and that is how I ended up in Real World Studios and ultimately how I met John. I was around thirty years old at this stage and I was down in Real World to record not just the classical repertoire with Nigel but because he was also working on an album for Stephen 'Tin Tin' Duffy [1993's *Music in Colour*]. That was the connection because Stephen hung out a lot with Sagat Guirey, who was the guitarist on the album, and he also knew Andrea Oliver and Michael Giri. At some point Sagat called me up and said, 'I don't know what you're doing at the weekend, but my friend John Reynolds is working with Andrea Oliver, and I've sort of bigged you up, so would you fancy coming down to his flat and playing the cello?' I said, 'Yeah, I'll do that!' My answer to things is basically 'Yes!' because if it scares me a bit then I'll do it. And I loved it. So, John and I started collaborating and we found it really easy to work together. He liked the style that I brought to string arranging; if I worked on a song I literally just made it up in my head and tracked the cello. He had a fantastic way of knowing that I was busy

building a chord, it wasn't going to be a solo line or something. We were sort of telepathic, he knew where I was going with it. And if you can imagine, this was in the ADAT [Alesis Digital Audio Tape] time. There was no digital, you literally had to wait for those spools to tighten. But even then, it was a very quick process and he had a lovely way of panning the cello, so it did actually sound like more than one cello on the recording.

Caroline would become an intrinsic part of Reynolds's recording and touring projects. Her association with Reynolds led to a particularly creative period, with her getting involved in more of the producer's output, including albums by Indigo Girls (*Come On Now Social*, 1999), Sinead O' Connor (*Faith and Courage*, 2000), Irish singer-songwriter Damien Dempsey (*Seize the Day*, 2003; *Shots*, 2005), not to mention the inception of their own band entitled Ghostland, which would go on to release two studio albums across five years: the eponymous debut *Ghostland* (1998) and their 2003 follow-up *Interview with an Angel*. The group's soulful widescreen sound incorporates Celtic, Classical, and Middle Eastern influences in creating its remarkably eclectic body of song.

After I began working with John it would be a normal thing for me to turn up to his place and he would say, 'here's a couple of tracks, could you possibly put some strings on?' It was just such an easy process. John and I had started working on various little things and then Ian Stanley, who was the pianist from Tears for Fears and who worked for EastWest Records, signed us and said, 'why don't you and John be in a band?' That's how Ghostland happened, which was me, John, and Justin Adams. I absolutely loved it, I got into World Music through that. We played together as a band before we became an official band with a name. My first tour with Sinead was in 1996, and it was a big American tour. Then on the following tour she decided to have Ghostland as her band, which was me, Clare [Kenny], Justin, and John, although at that point we hadn't actually been known as Ghostland yet. We did all the Lilith Fairs on that tour. I was new to it really, whereas Clare and John had gone back with Sinead for yonks and yonks. It started out as me, John, and Justin just basically jamming, working off little fragments of ideas, and what John is so good at is creating a base to it; he would hear something in the cello line or he would hear a groove that Justin had come up with, or it could come from a drum rhythm or a melody. So individually, or sometimes in twos or threes, we gradually created these demoes and then we fleshed them out. We actually went to Ian Stanley's place in Bath and spent a few weeks where Tears for Fears recorded *Songs from the Big Chair* and that was an intense period of time when we were fleshing it out. We brought in Natacha Atlas and various other singers would come along and play. Another one of those was Cara Dillon, who started the Frome Folk Festival. Cara was on the *Interview with an Angel* album, and I think we would all agree that we were less happy with that album. We just felt that it was like a watered-down version of us and a little bit too commercial. It just didn't work. I would rather have not sold any albums and just have something that was a bit more of us. I am happy with the string pieces that we were able to do though. But for various reasons we didn't have free rein on that one. On the first album we actually had a budget to bring in a few string players, which we recorded at John's place in Durham Terrace. We got eight string players down to John's to record and there was nowhere for them to sit. So, they were all sat on the corner of a table or wherever they could find space. It was a big room, but it wasn't massive, yet we somehow managed to record an orchestra for the album. On the second one we had the luxury of Abbey Road. But another thing about that time recording the second album was John being very ill with pneumonia, so everything was a little more fractured. There were some very nice things about it, but I would love to do a third one.

It was thanks to her work with Ghostland that the opportunity for a solo project was presented to Caroline. Rob Dickins, an executive from the band's record label EastWest (and former chairman of Warner Music UK) had been to see Caroline play the Elgar cello concerto at the Barbican in London when he conceived of the idea to commission a Caroline Dale solo record for Instant Karma Records. Caroline says,

Rob knew I had sort of stepped into both worlds, and he liked the idea of me writing and recording my own album. So, I did. And Rob assigned the project a budget of £30,000, which was brilliant! That meant not only could I do it at EMI, but I could have an orchestra, which is unheard of now. I was very lucky to be at the tail end of that time in the industry because when he wanted me to do a follow-up album there was no money, and it was just impossible to do it. But initially I thought, 'what am I going to write?' I decided not to do a whole album of my own stuff because I just didn't know if I was capable of doing it comprised entirely of original material, but I found myself suddenly getting inspiration out of nowhere, apart from the mild panic that I had to write something. So, I did what I normally do and just took off somewhere on my own. I just drove along the A1 not knowing where I was going to end up, I just had a keyboard and the cello in the back of the car, and I gave myself two weeks to come up with some idea of what I wanted. But as I was driving the car broke down and I ended up in the middle of this tiny village in Hertfordshire; I found a pub there and I just walked in with my cello and keyboard and said, 'Do you have a room for a couple of weeks?' and they said 'yeah!' I just looked like this odd woman playing away on my keyboard for a couple of weeks, but it just worked, I came up with some ideas that felt strong, and Rob really liked them. And that is how the album was spawned.

Such Sweet Thunder was released in 2002 and was comprised of original tracks and classical pieces by Vivaldi and Handel. It would prove to be a bittersweet moment for the musician, as she could finally present a work that made those six-hour trips to London for lessons with Florence Hooten worth the long haul down the motorway.

'It was lovely that my mum managed to hear the album', Caroline reveals.

She had Alzheimer's and my dad had just passed away. I still have images of mum and dad watching me play and I love that. It's the thing I'm most proud of, that they were there and were able to see me doing something. And it must have been tricky for them, not being from the pop world, to understand what their daughter was doing. They were probably thinking 'you're on this perfectly lovely classical train track route and you've just wandered!' But then they got it. Another lovely thing about the album was John Reynolds co-produced it, so he was there too. It felt like a culmination of everything.

Caroline brought several notable collaborators onto the album, including her sister Miranda Dale, noted cellist Phillip De Groote, and Pink Floyd frontman David Gilmour. Caroline had grown up in awe of Gilmour's work and had become socially acquainted with him through her friendship with film composer Michael Kamen. Then, while she was living in a cramped basement apartment in Notting Hill in the early 1990s, she received a phone call that would lead to the first of several professional associations with Gilmour.

The David Gilmore thing was a very strange one. Michael Kamen would always have these amazing Thanksgiving parties and all the A-listers would come and play, or some wouldn't play, they'd just turn up. So, that's how I got to kind of know David. But then at one stage I was living in Powis Terrace in Notting Hill in this little hovel and my friend Paolo from the band Sunhouse was living there, as was my big, tall friend Sophia, who was with Independiente [British independent record label]. I woke up one day and said to Paolo that we really need to paint my room, we've got to do something with it, and we've got to listen to some music while we're doing it. Back in those days there was Woolies – which was Woolworths – and we went to our nearest one and said, 'let's get *Wish You Were Here* by Pink Floyd!' So, we brought back that album and started painting and then someone ran in and said, 'You'll never guess what! This new book about Notting Hill, we're in it! "26 Powis Terrace is the site of the London Free School where the likes of Pink Floyd used to rehearse in the basement!"' And then the phone rings and it's David Gilmore! I was so shocked. I said to him that we were just painting and listening to *Wish You Were Here*, and I told him about this basement, and he confirmed that yes, they did rehearse there. But he was ringing me as he had been asked to do the Meltdown Festival at the South Bank which was curated by Robert Wyatt. David was asked to headline one night, and then Kate Bush played the second night and Bob Geldof did the third night. But he asked if I would be his cellist. It was just fantastic to rehearse every day in this little clubhouse in the middle of East Sussex.

The Meltdown Festival is an annual series of concerts that are curated by a different notable musician every year, and it takes place at London's Royal Festival Hall. Caroline performed at the festival with Gilmour in June 2001. This was the beginning of a professional relationship that would see Gilmour contributing an original song called 'Babbie's Daughter' to *Such Sweet Thunder*. In turn, Caroline would provide cello for three songs on Gilmour's 2006 solo album, *On an Island*.

It was lovely that David played on my album. Around that time, he had written something called 'Babbie's Daughter' and I did a sort of B-section to it, so he came in and played that and it's on the album. I'm very lucky to meet my heroes. It meant a lot to be able to work with David. I was that misunderstood fourteen-year-old – or I thought I was misunderstood because I was fourteen, you know. I was listening to *Dark Side of the Moon* with my friends, and I thought I was misunderstood by my parents. My overriding experience with David, once he called me up, was going down to his farm, sitting there with him, and him saying to me, 'what do you want to do on this?' Then he would kick out this iconic chord or start playing 'Shine on You Crazy Diamond'; there he was with his foot pedal, playing his guitar, and I honestly thought I'd gone to heaven. It was just the most magical synergy of everything, it's like you've just seen your life flashing before your eyes. And with Kate Bush as well, one of my overriding memories is of 'Moments of Pleasure', which I think is one of her best tracks, but Michael Kamen had done this fantastic arrangement for it that we were playing in Abbey Road and there was Kate Bush listening and Michael conducting us through this incredible piece, and I just thought 'I'm the luckiest woman ever!'

With a CV already comprised of music's biggest acts – Oasis, Jimmy Page, Robert Plant, Charlie Watts, David Gilmour, Heart – Caroline's skills would continue to be sought out by the industry's heavy hitters, not to mention an obscure beat combo from Dublin. 'And then there was U2! That came about through Brian Eno asking me to play on something and I did this layered cello thing which Bono really liked, so I started doing some compositions for them'. Those compositions would end up on the band's twelfth studio album, *No Line on the Horizon* (2009), and would lead to further work with the quartet on their subsequent long player, *Songs of Innocence* (2014), as well as providing arrangements for various live shows.

U2 were fantastic people to work with, they are all lovely. And I also worked with David Gray, it has been absolutely wonderful to work with him over the years; that has been really special. And I got to do the strings on albums for Joan Armatrading and Belinda Carlisle. They are the nicest, the most genuine people. To me it feels as though there is no particular script to it all. I think if there was advice that I could give it would be to just say 'yes' and go to where you're not quite sure what's going to happen and just trust your instinct. I know if I was to go play jazz that I would be crap at it, but I was in a Balanescu Quartet which involved improvising and it did feel like jumping off a cliff. I didn't know what I was doing but I was just doing it anyway; I was realizing that if you don't die doing it, something will come out. But coming from the classical background, a lot of people have that fear of taking away the dots. It is a much simpler thing to do if I'm backing Page and Plant or David Gilmour; it's not as technical, but you do have to keep those little muscles in gear, so alongside all these big rock gigs, I did keep the classical thing going with the English Chamber Orchestra.

In recent years, Caroline has contributed to the soundtracks of many Hollywood blockbusters, working with the likes of Michael Giacchino (on *Jurassic World Dominion*), Hans Zimmer (on *Wonder Woman 1984*), Danny Elfman (on *Dumbo*), and Mark Mothersbaugh (on *Thor: Ragnarok*). Caroline was introduced to film work by Barrington Pheloung, an Australian composer who was the musical director of the London Contemporary Dance Theatre during her time there. Pheloung is perhaps most well-known for his theme tune to the ITV drama series *Inspector Morse*, and in 1990 he was hired by former *Morse* writer and future Oscar-winning Hollywood director Anthony Minghella to score his debut feature film, *Truly, Madly, Deeply*. That film proved to be the first in a prolific line of work in film music for Caroline, for which she credits Pheloung and her time in the Contemporary Dance Theatre.

'I really got into soundtrack work through Barrington, who sadly passed away a couple of years ago', she affirms.

> Just as I was starting out and doing the Contemporary Dance thing, he had begun getting various gigs in the studio and one of those that he got was *Inspector Morse*, which was a very popular television programme back in the day. Then he got *Truly, Madly, Deeply* and how he got that is because Anthony Minghella had directed one of the *Inspector Morse* episodes. I remember talking to Anthony about it and he said that because he was a writer and not yet a director, he was worried about cutting his teeth on something like an *Inspector Morse* programme, but then he had been given the opportunity to direct *Truly, Madly, Deeply* after he had written it. I think that was his feature debut. So, then he approached Barry to do the soundtrack because he knew him from *Inspector Morse*, so Barry did the music for the film, and he brought me in to work on it. I then had to teach Alan Rickman – well, not *had to*, I loved it – but I had to teach Alan Rickman the cello for it, just as I had to teach Emily Watson the cello for *Hilary and Jackie*. I still absolutely love *Truly Madly, Deeply*. And of course, it wasn't originally called *Truly, Madly, Deeply*, it started out as something called *Cello* for the BBC2 *Play for Today* anthology show, but then it was changed. I found this out when I was with this piano trio that I started out in New York; I used to commute over there quite a bit and one day the pianist in the trio said, 'Hey, I heard you in this amazing film called *Truly, Madly, Deeply*', and I said, 'I don't know what you're talking about!' The BBC had sold it to America and that's where they re-titled it.

This supernatural romantic melodrama set in leafy middle-class Highgate involves a grief-stricken translator named Nina (Juliet Stevenson) who struggles to move on from the death of her recently deceased musician boyfriend, Jamie (Alan Rickman). Her overwhelming sadness is somewhat abated when Jamie's restless spirit returns from the afterlife to live with his lost love. The pair rekindle the relationship to the degree that they can, which, admittedly, is not a lot. So, it isn't long before Nina meets an irritatingly quirky art therapist, Mark (Michael Maloney), and falls for his awkward charms, leaving Jamie to move on to the afterlife in peace. In his mortal life, Jamie was a brilliant cellist, and the hands and sounds of the cello in the film are those of Caroline Dale.

Pheloung would prove to be the crucial connection for Caroline coming aboard another important film project, a job that would afford her the opportunity to pay further tribute to the art and influence of her hero Jacqueline du Pré for Anand Tucker's 1998 biographical film, *Hilary and Jackie*. After winning some bureaucratic Hollywood battles over the hiring of the musician who would be performing Du Pré's pieces, Pheloung, the film's composer, knew well that Caroline could channel her great influence for the screen and so he duly brought her in to work on the soundtrack. The narrative of the film focuses on the fractured relationship between Jacqueline and her flautist sister, Hilary, respectively played by Emily Watson and Emily Griffith. The film depicts the tension that mounted between the sibling musicians as Jacqueline's natural virtuosity led to international prominence which belied her earlier disregard for practice and academia, while the dedicated Hilary struggled through her musical studies. The discord between the pair is further exacerbated by Jacqueline's sexual interest in Hilary's husband, Christopher 'Kiffer' Finzi.

> How I came to that film was just something of a weird coincidence, or perhaps not a coincidence. Indeed, it was a variety of different pointers which contrived to get me to do *Hilary and Jackie*. Barry [Pheloung] was the connection to me working on that film. When the project came to him, he was asked to do the music and he said he wanted me to work on it. And obviously because it was a big Hollywood thing – it being funded with Hollywood money – all the people over there wanted some American cellist, which I think was Yo-Yo Ma. [Sony Classical chief] Peter Gelb was the head of whatever it was, and he was just gunning for his American guy. So, there were a lot of people pulling it apart, but Barry stuck with me and so did the producer, who had come to know me through a different connection. The producer and Barry both said, 'We must have Caroline Dale!' so eventually this guy Peter Gelb said, 'Oh, well we just have to hire her then'. But it was an amazing experience to study your hero like that, and there was a huge amount of repertoire to learn; I had learnt it before anyway, but I had learnt it as me, so to re-learn it through her fingers and bowings, it was absolutely fascinating. And it was chronologically fascinating too because I had to play her as a young girl and then I had to play her as she was beginning to have MS, so it was almost like an acting challenge through the cello. So, getting to work on *Hilary and Jackie* really came through a lot of different angles.

Caroline's work for the silver screen has been prolific and acclaimed, working repeatedly with composers such as Dario Marianelli, Thomas Newman, and Alberto Iglesias. Her playing can be heard in some of the biggest blockbusters in recent times, but the most celebrated moment of that work was perhaps Marianelli's Academy Award win for Best Original Score for *Atonement* at the 80th Oscar ceremony in 2008.

> I've been the solo cellist on many films and there are some compos-
> ers who are just brilliant to work with and I have done so on several
> occasions. One of those would be Dario Marianelli. I met Dario on
> *Pride and Prejudice*, that was the first one I did with him, and I did
> *Atonement* with him and that was a big one for me. I was doing a
> very classical Wigmore Hall concert where I did Shostakovich and
> also a Debussy sonata and it got me thinking that it would be lovely
> to do the world premiere of something there, and I had just done
> the cello for *Atonement* so I asked Dario if he would be willing to
> compose a cello and piano suite to play at the Wigmore Hall and
> he said 'yeah, I would love to do that!' And then he got the Oscar
> for that score! So, it was a really nice thing to be able to perform
> the music from the film. Dario is such a talent. Another composer
> I love working with is Tom Newman. I did *1917* with him; I was
> the solo cellist on that. That was a beautiful movie, but it was also
> a very beautiful soundtrack. And then there's Alberto Iglesias who
> I've been doing all the Pedro Almodovar soundtracks with over
> the years. Getting to collaborate with all those great composers is
> just fantastic.

In the age of increased secrecy and non-disclosure agreements due to
incessant internet inquisitiveness and everything else that comes with the
digital exploitation of commercial art, it has become increasingly hard for
Caroline to be privy to a complete cut of the film she is expected to emote to,
and thus perform to.

'There's so many NDAs floating around these days that you very rarely get
to see the film you are scoring', she reveals.

> In the old days we had the film on the screen in front of us the
> whole time, but these days you are very lucky to be able to see
> anything that you are tracking to. Harry Gregson-Williams is an
> exception, he will always have the film up. If you are doing a solo
> for someone like Harry or Dario, it is really important for me to
> see what I'm playing to. On *1917* I actually got the chance to fol-
> low the scenes as I was playing the solo. So, the music is often
> pre-written, but you can put different colours to the picture as you
> are seeing it, if you are lucky to be able to have the footage there.
> I love being able to react to it and do something slightly different
> within the confines of what they've written. They normally have
> to demo everything with a synth cello, so you hope you are better
> than that; it would be bad if they kept the synth after you came in

to play. We've all done those sessions where you have to play one long note again and again each a different way. But string solos don't work on synths, luckily.

After the Covid-19 pandemic shut down the livelihoods of musicians across the globe, Caroline found herself in isolation longing to be back working with the dots. After the restrictions were eased, live performances made a tentative return and musicians began to find work once again, so Caroline embraced the moment to be as prolific as ever. While soundtrack work has been a constant in Caroline's career, she has found time to return to the road as the guest principal with the Academy of St. Martin in the Fields. When the panic around the pandemic began to subside, Caroline played her first prom back in the summer of 2021 with the Academy; it was a mixture of Vivaldi's *The Four Seasons* and *The Four Seasons of Buenos Aires* by Astor Piazzolla. With further tours coming up in the United States, Germany, and Spain, as well as concerts planned with the English Chamber Orchestra, with whom Caroline has been principal cellist for eighteen years, she will be reunited with the audience whose feedback and emotional response the musician feeds off.

> I do love live work, that's one of the things a lot of musicians have missed during the lockdown. I missed the energy you get from the audience. You can do all these streamed gigs from your home and pretend that there is somebody listening, and I'm sure there are, but it's not the same as having somebody in the room picking up on the energy of the music. The Academy of St. Martin are a lovely orchestra, and its MD is Joshua Bell, the violinist, who is just a fantastic hero of mine, and we're doing some dates with a wonderful violinist named Julia Fisher. The isolation of not being able to be around other musicians or be in the same room as anyone was the worst. But once studio work came back, I was a) grateful because it was work, and b) I missed the challenge of that, which I love.

As for further excursions into solo work to follow *Such Sweet Thunder*, Caroline has been somewhat reticent about the idea, fearing to appear egotistical. Despite such reluctance, she does tease that further collaboration with her old Ghostland comrade John Reynolds is something in her sights. She ponders,

> I might do another solo project, but it's not something I've considered much because sometimes those things feel like a vanity project. Despite that feeling, you do get to an age where you go 'if not now, when?' You either do it or you don't. I wonder if it is the fear of wanting to be as good as possible that stops me or is it because I'm thinking 'oh, that's just a vanity project'. But then there are a few

things that I would like to commit to record. I have labelled some time with John to get in the studio and start writing. We really want to do something and that is high on my list. It just feels like it needs to be done, there's something in there that we feel we have to get out. It's interesting, I was just speaking to John today and he said to me, 'Nobody buys albums anymore, and that actually gives you a huge freedom'. That is true, because it doesn't have to sell, it doesn't need to fulfil any criteria that there should be a hit or there should be a hook; that's all gone out the window. You can do exactly what you like because it could sell as little as you like; with no commercial expectations comes huge artistic freedom. We've got rid of our various mortgages and things like that, so it feels much freer now to be able to just express oneself as you want to. With there being no budgets anymore, you really can do anything. The old industry rules no longer exist. You can cut your cloth because there isn't any expectation, it is just a matter of collaborating with the people that you really want to work with because there's nobody telling you not to anymore. There's no record company breathing down your neck and saying, 'It should sound like this', there's just nothing now. There's nothing to stop us, darling!

9 Angie Pollock

Rewind to Scotland's Midland Valley sometime in the mid-1970s. The Pollock family are at church and song is in the air when a curious little girl takes notice that her mother is singing differently to those around her. 'I'm harmonizing, Angie', Ellie Pollock says to her enquiring daughter. Singing was nothing unusual in this family. In fact, it was an elemental part of their life.

'Everyone sang!' the now adult Angie enthuses.

> I started singing when I was around two or three, in church and with my family, with harmony. It was a huge part of my childhood; music was always in the family. We used to have a thing called the 'Von Craps', where we did four-part harmony, Elvis – 'Wise Men Say' and some other nice things that got added as we got older like Carole King – 'Will You Love Me Tomorrow'. We knew where the other one had to fit harmonically and if you treaded on somebody's melodic toes you either had to both move at the same time, or somebody had to find another part. It was a natural thing and we had loads of fun singing together, in the car or after dinner… wherever. My Granddad had perfect pitch, and my dad has too. My Mum has a beautiful voice. I think when you are little it rubs off on you more than you realize. Everyone in my family played, and I started when I was roughly six. Mum sings as I mentioned, especially Rabbie Burns which was her favourite; also, she used to play piano even although she begs to differ now. When she was younger, she used to enter singing competitions. My dad 'Bob' can play pretty much anything he picks up. He had a drumkit. When my parents got married my mum made him choose. I think it affected the ambience of the lounge! We had a massive xylophone in the garage at that time, but I was too young to appreciate it but still had a plonk on it now and again. Both of my grandfathers (Papas) had

organs. Papa Carle a Hammond organ and Papa Pollock a Farfisa – I had loads of fun on those as a kid. Papa Carle also let me play his Elvis vinyl collection from a very young age... I loved it. My second piano teacher was in Scotland. Edith Ferguson – she was incredible, and I adored her.

Angie was born in Greenock, Scotland, but grew up in the historic county of Lanarkshire, before the family moved to Hertfordshire in England when she was turning eleven. Having grown up in such musical environs, it was perhaps inevitable that Angie would at least try her hand at working in the industry. A crucial break came about in 1993 whilst employed at a recording studio as a tape-op, or a 'go-for', as Angie would say. On her third week working there she met former Specials frontman Terry Hall, who was at the facility writing and recording demos for his solo debut *Home* along with ex-Smiths guitarist Craig Gannon. Angie says,

> I was in my teens, I was still living at home in Hertfordshire with my family. I had a great time with those guys; they were all really sweet and I was extremely green! I ended up doing a few bits and bobs on that demo and then I went on my first tour with Terry for his first album. And from there I toured with him on and off. Terry Hall was pretty big at the time. I loved his voice, and he was great to sing with; we recorded the album in Liverpool with Ian Broudie producing. When I started with Terry and Craig it was a DAT machine that we used live. Then we were joined by Les Pattinson from Echo and the Bunnymen on bass and Chris Sharrock on drums. With Terry we did quite a bit of TV and radio promo and a lot of touring. We supported Dave Stewart on a European tour. I remember jamming 'Here Comes the Rain Again' with Dave in the big room upstairs at Church Studios (Crouch End) as we were all rehearsing there, the two bands. That tour was a bigger production than I had been on. I learnt quite a lot in those days. I was a bit of a fish out of water, but the guys were amazingly cool. RIP, Terry. You are always in my heart.

Angie's next major step was made with another Dave Stewart and Terry Hall connection. Hall's management company also had Stewart's wife Siobhan Fahey on their roster, and it was with her group Shakespears Sister that Angie would embark on tour in 1994. Shakespears Sister experienced its greatest commercial success as a joint endeavour (with Fahey in collaboration with American co-singer Marcella Detroit) with the album *Hormonally Yours* (1992), but in the midst of industry and public approbation relations became contentious. Soon Shakespears Sister reverted to its original incarnation as a solo project for Fahey and she duly began assembling a touring band for a 1996 tour for the album *#3*.

> This was the version of the group without Marcy [Marcella Detroit] and they needed a keyboard player. All the band were Scottish funnily. We did some promo and a short tour, including playing a few festivals like T in the Park, which used to be held in my hometown in Scotland, and Pride festival in London. After that a few things came up.

Among those things that came up was the beginning of a fruitful professional relationship with Ian Broudie, the producer of Terry Hall's album *Home*. Angie made an impression on the former Original Mirrors and Big in Japan man, who was also several years deep into his Lightning Seeds band project, so when it came time to record the Lightning Seeds fourth album, *Dizzy Heights* (1996), Broudie brought in Angie to record vocals. The album would bring together various people from *Home*, including Hall and Sharrock. What began as a modest solo project for Broudie had by now become a full band situation which battled its way through the heady Britpop movement, a curious period which often seemed less concerned with the quality of bands emerging and more involved with the attendant culture war between Blur and Oasis. But the music of The Lightning Seeds would be heard amongst the din after they made their formidable contribution to Cool Britannia with their era-defining football anthem, 'Three Lions (It's Coming Home)'. It was during that period in which Angie became a regular part of the Lightning Seeds live line-up, and she continued to contribute to the band's recorded output as they came out the far side of Britpop with their dignity intact. Angie says,

> The Lightning Seeds was quite inter-linked through all the same people. Ian asked me to do some vocals on *Dizzy Heights* and from there I toured with The Lightning Seeds for quite a long time. I was part of that world constantly for about five years or more, and occasionally working with other people in between, like an odd thing with Terry or whatever cropped up. I'm lucky to have been there and to have continued to work with them over the years. The line-up did change with the amazing Zak Starkey stepping in on drums, which was a true delight and a pocket I thoroughly enjoyed sitting in. And of course, we had Martyn Campbell on bass, so it was a rhythm section from heaven. I played on the album *Tilt* in 1999 and I love that, it's one of my favourites. And I did some vocals for Ian on the Seeds record, *See You in the Stars*. They have loyal fans to this day. Ian has a great legacy of work behind him. The Lightning Seeds played *TFI Friday* with Chris Evans so many times it became something to look forward to doing. You had the

best fun on that show, and you'd be upset if you weren't playing there on a Friday night.

Angie continues,

> When Blur and Oasis were battling it out in the mainstream it was hard not to notice it, even though all that sort of thing blew over my head really because we were just so busy and having an amazing journey. We were full-on with touring or doing promo, and that's all you think about at the time. But that rivalry between those other Britpop bands was a thing of its own. This was a time when airplay was so important as people were still going to the shops to buy singles. Although it still is important, it's just different now. Back then it was great starting a tour and performing new songs which were becoming more familiar to the audience as the tour went on; it was a lovely thing to see. I was also growing up musically, surrounded by this incredible force of nature with these brilliant songs, musicians and people whom I still love dearly, it was one of the biggest learning curves of my life that I hold very sacred and it scared the bejesus out of me at the same time. It was an amazing time in music, great stuff was happening. We played this festival in Glasgow, and it was Mazzy Star, Radiohead, who were there with *The Bends*, Beck was there with *Odelay*, Pulp had *Different Class* going, you just couldn't move quick enough to catch all these great bands. Though I do remember a few years later stopping on my way to the shower in my pjs from the tour bus, to catch Polyphonic Spree followed by Arcade Fire, with my toilet bag under one arm and towel under the other. That's what I love about festivals.

At the turn of the millennium, Angie was not just busy recording with The Lightning Seeds but engaged in touring with Sophie Ellis-Bextor. It was during this time that a major opportunity arose which would end up being an important career move. It was whilst in rehearsal for an upcoming tour with the popstar that Angie heard Goldfrapp were auditioning for musicians, which piqued her interest immediately, as she recalls:

> I was rehearsing with Sophie Ellis-Bextor and the band for further UK and Europe dates at The Depot when I auditioned with Goldfrapp right across the street at John Henry's. I managed to finish Sophie's rehearsal in time to pop over there to meet Goldfrapp for the first time. They were starting their tour right after Sophie's tour finished so the timing was perfect. It doesn't always work out like that. We had a lovely tour over a couple of months with Sophie, then I began with Goldfrapp.

For Angie, it was the beginning of a long, rewarding professional engagement which took in worldwide tours and major festivals along the way as Goldfrapp went from acclaimed cult electronic duo with *Felt Mountain* (2000) to Top 20 chart act with *Black Cherry* (2003). It was for the tour in support of the latter album on which Angie would hit the road with a band that included bassist Charlie Jones, drummer Rowan Oliver, and Italian violinist Davide Rossi. With Goldfrapp being very much a studio concern, with all the music written, recorded, and produced by the duo of Alison Goldfrapp and Will Gregory, the challenge for Angie and her bandmates was to recreate it live. For music that is very much a soundscape, it is not just a case of grabbing the guitars and amps and saying, 'let's go!'

> Alison and Will are an incredible band and we [the musicians] join in when they go out live or they need a certain instrument on an album, but the band is the two of them. It can be complicated to recreate the music precisely, but it is important to keep the songs as they are. Although things do occasionally change depending on what is happening in the show. I think when you are a 'let's go' guitar band there might be a bit more of an element of freedom – but each artist is different as each band is. I haven't been with many bands that change things that radically live. Occasionally an intro or an outro or a specific emphasis or section for show reasons. These sounds and parts are there for important reasons, painstaking decisions, ingredients… and generally you play them as is! Even better when you can take sounds off the masters. I love triggering samples as much as I love sitting and playing the piano, but it is a different type of playing. You are playing most nights live but with the same repetition. In my world, there's less improv on stage. You are also discombobulated when you come home from a tour, so it's good to have something to get your head into and your hands. With triggering and all that type of playing, you must have enough preparation in advance because it's not always logical or natural to play. Sometimes you program the samples just to squeeze them on to whatever notes were left on the keyboard. Just to be able to cover more parts.

For much of 2003 the Black Cherry tour would roll through the United States, Canada, Europe, and the UK, before continuing the following year in Australia and Japan. The stage show would be an audio-visual extravaganza, spearheaded by frontwoman Alison Goldfrapp's unique artistic aesthetic when it comes to costuming and lighting. 'Alison has a vision', Angie applauds,

> she truly does, and it evolves and changes from album to album depending on the music. Sometimes that involves different

musicians on tour as well, so the line-up has slightly changed over the years to support the music and textures. It's always a lovely vibe on stage, and there is definitely a family element to it. After playing on stage and being on a tour for so long, over many years, it does become a family. It is important because that support is needed on and off stage. It is a comfort. You become dear friends and I truly love them.

Whenever Alison Goldfrapp and Will Gregory are locked away in the country writing and recording their albums, Angie continues to work with other artists and on other projects. Whether it is recording sessions, writing, or returning to the Lightning Seeds fold for festival shows, Angie prefers to keep busy. Sometimes, that involves local gigs in London; other times, major concerts with Peter Gabriel. 'It was really being around the Real World Studios that I met some people in that family', she says.

Things moved towards playing with Peter at some point following the work I had done at that studio on the album for a beautiful singer and artist called Tara Chinn. The album was recorded by the fantastic Richard Evans (with whom I have collaborated and worked on various projects since then) and featured co-writer/ guitarist Tony Fennell, bassist Tony Levin, and drummer Ged Lynch. Real World is wonderful place to record. The Bosendorfer piano was up on the top floor. I just fell in love with that piano. I have done a few tours with those guys, most recently with Peter and Sting sharing headline in America. That was an incredible tour, with both bands being on stage for the majority of the show. A real dream to play.

Angie continues,

I did a tour and some promo with Brett Anderson from Suede on one of his solo albums, *Slow Attack*, which was a more piano-driven gig. I also did a lot of vocals for my late friend Neil Brockbank, who had a studio in Clapham called Gold Top Studios, which used to be in Camden. It was a magical studio to work at and had a great gang of artists and musicians who hung out there. I met Neil as he did front of house on a few Lightning Seeds festival gigs years ago and he asked me if I wanted to sing on some records that he was making. Neil recorded very old school, so it was a joy to be working with him and his assistant Tuck Nelson, and the late Bobby Trehern, who was an incredible drummer and amazing character to be with. Neil and Bobby were best friends and a team, and I spent a good bit of time in the studio with them on different projects in between touring, a really special time. I was also on the *QM2* with Chris Difford who brought together some very talented writers and musicians. We mentored passengers over a short crossing from Southampton to New York and by the end of the crossing the passengers had written and recorded their song/s. They also performed them in the Queens room on the ship to the other passengers, with a bit of encouragement from us. It was such a beautiful thing, camaraderie between the mentors, the whole experience. Though we did get caught in a gale force 11 petering 12 storm in the middle of the Atlantic and one of the engines caught on fire. That was wild.

Further work came along for Angie when she collaborated with Badly Drawn Boy, on the song 'Let It Rain' which was written and recorded for inclusion on the 2012 soundtrack for the Robert De Niro film, *Being Flynn*. 'I have always been a huge fan of Damon's music', she admits, 'he and Steve McLaughlin were working on the music for this DeNiro film. For me it was a little stint but quite special'. In between other tours, Angie hit the road with erstwhile Ash guitarist Charlotte Hatherley for her solo work. 'I think we laughed as much as we played', Angie says, before adding, 'I also played with Karl Hyde from Underworld on his solo debut album *Edgeland*. Karl's a gem to work with and it was a lovely set up. Touring included, Japan, Australia, Europe including some very cool festivals and venues!'

Angie went on to work on a rather unique project in 2012 with Bristol-based bassist Gaz Williams. *Pop'pea* was a 'rock opera' reinterpretation of Monteverdi's *L'incoronazione di Poppea*, staged at Théâtre du Châtelet in Paris and starring Soft Cell's Marc Almond and The Libertines' Carl Barât. This multimedia event wasn't Angie's typical gig, but it was a memorable one, as she recalls:

It was the original Monteverdi topline, plus guitar-driven arrangements; a mixture of analogue and live drums. It was this wild, fantastic rock opera with a fabulous crew of singing and acting cast members. The production involved musicians, circus performers, miming, film, animation, technical stage designs, and operatic choir. The whole thing was a real melting pot of performers and technical artists across the spectrum. I was pulled in last minute and we could virtually watch the first performance getting closer and closer but somehow it all came together in a short space of time, with everyone working so hard to make it happen. I also returned home from this trip with a puppy named Poppy, who was found around the corner from Le Châtelet and needed to be rescued.

Little did Parisian Poppy realize that this chance encounter with the visiting musician would lead to a new home and an auspicious recording debut. Joining Angie in the studio one day, Poppy's backing, or perhaps, barking vocals, ended up on Geraint Watkins's song 'Mosquito'. Angie admits,

> That song has a very special place in my heart, and that's because while we were recording, Poppy decided to howl when I had left her in the live room alone for five minutes. I had gone into the mixing room to join Neil and Geraint to check my vocals. As it turned out, Poppy had impeccable timing and so they decided to keep her performance on the record. A tough negotiation of dog treats was agreed, and Poppy was very happy.

In 2014 Angie received a phone call inviting her on tour with former Thompson Twins frontman Tom Bailey, who was returning to the live circuit after a twenty-seven-year hiatus. With a catalogue of 1980s hits to dispense, she couldn't resist the offer. 'You can't beat those songs', she affirms, 'really – "Hold Me Now"?! It was wonderful to be performing those songs'. The touring band consisted of Angie, keyboardist Amanda Kramer, and drummer Emily Dolan Davies; it was a rare but not entirely uncommon instance of an all-female band backing a male solo artist. When it came to replicating the Thompson Twins catalogue live, the band's approach proved to be a satisfyingly physical one for the musicians. Rather than relying unnecessarily on tracks, the various keyboards parts were divided up between the players. After deciding what should and shouldn't be played, they each chose various piano and string parts which were performed for real. Angie recalls,

> A lot of it was on track, we had these little onstage monitor systems with separate channels, so we all controlled our own live sound. I remember mine being pretty loud, but I like to play in the middle of everything. I only had a couple of sounds that had rhythmic elements on the sound delay-wise or whatever, but the majority of it was playing the parts we wanted to cover that made sense for us to play live. We had no triggers; we physically played everything. And there was quite a bit of singing involved. And Tom was jumping from guitar to keyboards to drums then percussion, and vocals of course. We had a great time on and off stage. Tom is a real gem.

After years of studio work providing keyboards and vocals for various acts, Angie put her recording experience to use in 2016 when she co-produced Tanita Tikaram's jazz-infused ninth album, *Closer to the People*. Angie was approached to co-produce the album with Goetz Botzenhardt after she played some shows with Tikaram in 2015.

Bobby Trehern and Tanita asked me to work live on some festival shows, then following that Tanita asked me to work on her album with her. I was co-producing on the arranging, the Musical Director side of things. My job was to think outside of the box really. Mainly just coming up with any ideas and directions for the songs. Tanita and I were initially introduced through Neil Brockbank and Bobby, who was Tanita's drummer. Neil had also produced Tanita before. We worked closely together, so it was a joint effort between the three of us doing arrangements or working on sounds, parts, backing vocals, harmonies, whatever was needed really. Just trying to play around with the songs and figure out what worked best. From the perspective of being a female producer, it was nice to be working with a female artist in that scenario. I would definitely say that Tanita filled me with a lot of confidence, in an area I had worked less in. As did Goetz. He is a very talented mixing engineer as well as a very creative producer. Technically brilliant. I would work on sounds, or parts through the night sometimes, after a day in the studio to take in the next day. He was always open and able to interpret any ideas no matter how bonkers or possibly annoying.

Angie continues,

Even though it was just the three of us mainly working on it, there was of course mega input from some of the players, all of whom had worked with Neil, Bobby, and Tanita before – Martin Winning, Matt Radford, Matt Holland, Oliver Darling. Martin played a huge role not only with his writing and his musical performance, but he was also always massively helpful with his ears and thoughts when needed. Matt plays double bass with Tanita live and he also writes with her – I love the song they wrote and performed together, 'My Enemy'. 'Night is a Bird' is one I also love from the experimental side of things and was so much fun to record with everyone. I enjoyed the routine of being in the studio every day and working with them, it was a great period. I was very happy in that bubble. As was my dog Poppy, who got to come to work with me every day.

Like many musicians in the past few years, whether by necessity or by desire, Angie's home has become her creative salon. From there she has been kept busy, or perhaps sane, as despite the lockdown limbo of the last three years she has juggled a variety of projects that encompass film, art, and charitable endeavours, all within a musical context. A connection from her work with Peter Gabriel led to her work on a short film called *Otis' Dream*. The project was written by Pastor Otis Moss III to tell the story of his grandfather Otis Moss, Sr., a Southern black farmer who was denied his dream to vote in

1946 and died before ever having the opportunity to exercise his democratic right. Angie says,

> Dickie Chappell, the main person that I interfaced with over my many years working with Peter Gabriel, he was the right-hand man when it came down to anything musical. I would always work directly with Dickie, to get the sounds right and all the samples right when we were getting ready for the touring. Dickie was approached by his long-term friend Malcolm Du Plessis, who is from South Africa and is currently working in Nashville with Common Hymnal, an organization based in Nashville supporting left-field Christianity to help them write Christian poetry and songs, from a praise and protest point of view. It's a record company, so it is music-based but with lots of visual arts attached. Common Hymnal were approached by a film organization to work on a project called *Otis' Dream*, which was sponsored by Oprah Winfrey in encouraging African Americans to go out and vote. The Spirituals made a choir recording and I collaborated with them to put some piano on there. Dickie helped produce the track and it got used on the outro of the film.

Further remote recording work came her way when she was contacted by Tim Oliver of Real World Studios, who drafted in Angie to contribute piano and vocals for a new Damien Dempsey track. Angie reveals,

> I had been a fan of Damien Dempsey for a few years, and so this was certainly something that I loved working on throughout the pandemic. The song was called 'What a Day' and was produced by John Reynolds. It was recently chosen by Brian Eno to be part of his release of 100 new and unreleased tracks that he chose from 100 artists for his [music industry climate change charity initiative] Earth Percent to coincide with Earth Day. You could listen and/or donate over a time and hear any tracks you wanted.

She continues, revealing a particular moment of calm and connection in this most isolated time:

> Dave Spiers, who is an incredible keyboard player and friend, contacted me during the beginning of Covid-lockdown to get involved with his Isolation Choir. This was a beautiful way of pulling people together who were in isolation. He took our separate voices to create a new synth patch, which was given the name 'Isolation Choir'. I can't quite explain the feeling when I listened to what we had made, but it was a very magical and emotional moment in a horrendous

cloud – everything stopped for something beautiful, which is what we all needed during that time!

Other projects have allowed Angie to incorporate her love of animation by developing a multimedia workload that includes music videos for her own songs, as well as others, and quirky short subjects that parlay her wicked sense of humour into something visually arresting. Angie affirms,

> Things seem to be moving towards a home-based creative life, especially during the last couple of years. I had to take a bit of time out of touring due to suffering from long-covid; and being asthmatic, it hit me pretty hard. I am not saying I won't tour again but I am enjoying the process of creativity as much. I love animating and have been self-taught. To me it goes hand in hand with music and gives me a creative outlet. It started from my collage artwork, and it eventually got to the point where I wanted to make things move. I started experimenting and learning from there. I had put a couple of things up on YouTube, one called 'Loveforsale'. Then a couple of random animations like 'He11 yeh' where I already had written the Halloween music, so I ordered a couple of skeletons from Amazon and had a bit of fun with it. I also like using objects as well as random cut-outs from old pictures I have gathered over the years…

She continues,

> I then made a couple of videos for singer-songwriter Athena Andreadis, whom I had written with in the past. I also recorded a version of 'Scarborough Fair' with Chris Moorhead and made an animation for that. It's an on-going passion and something I want to continue doing. I recently put out a new track called 'Riders'. Kate St. John wrote a beautiful string arrangement which was performed by the Q-Strings. I tend to always be working on something and recently started making NFTs [non-fungible tokens] which I am putting up or 'dropping' as we speak. As long as I am being creative in some sort of art form, I am quite happy. If it feels right at the time, then I put it out. I always have some ideas bubbling away that I'm working on for myself. Never say never.

10 Sue Hadjopoulos

It is midwinter in Midtown, 1982. A young musician is racing through the streets to get to an audition. Her scarf billows in the icy wind as she pushes a shopping cart transporting her tools for the job: a pair of bongos. She is rolling her money maker to a Manhattan recording studio hoping to land a gig with an artist who anonymously advertised for additional musicians in *The Village Voice* – 'Major recording artist seeks percussionist: congas, bongos, timbales, mallets'. She was alerted to the notice by a friend who insisted on her making the call, even though she didn't play mallets. After some back and forth with the mystery artist's manager, including answering a line of inquiry about her Latin music credentials, the curious musician eventually discovered just who she would be trying out for: Joe Jackson. Unfamiliar with the British new waver's brand of eclectic sophisti-pop, she set out to her local record store for a crash course in the artist's oeuvre. Apply for the job, then study. This has been a recurring theme in the career of Sue Hadjopoulos, and, evidently, it has worked out exquisitely. Sue says,

> I finally got to the studio, and normally when you go in for an audition there's somebody at the desk to greet you, but I got there and didn't see anybody. So, I just went bursting into the room and the only people in there was Joe and another guy on the keyboard. So, in my beautiful New York accent, I go, 'Oh, hi Joe! How are ya? How ya doin'? I'm Sue!' And he turns, pauses, and looks at me like a doe caught in headlights. He just didn't know what to make of that and he says, 'Would you mind waiting outside?' He wasn't being mean or anything, just a bit surprised. 'Oh yeah, sure', I say, 'no problem!' and I roll back out.

It may have been an awkward and inauspicious introduction, but as Sue retreated to the waiting area, little did she realize that by the end of the day she would leave a musical impression upon Jackson that marked the beginning of a professional relationship that spanned thirty years. This early association with Jackson got Sue noticed by all the right people in the music industry, leading to her becoming a highly sought-after percussionist for recording sessions and major world tours. For the past forty-five years, Sue has been bringing her flavour of Latin rhythm to artists as diverse as Simple Minds, Cyndi Lauper, David Byrne, Laurie Anderson, The B-52s, and many more across a wide variety of genres. The rhythm for which she is justly celebrated runs through the Hadjopoulos blood, as she discovered her passion for playing whilst being brought up in a musical family headed by her Greek father and Puerto Rican mother. Born in Queens, New York, and raised in Long Island, Sue was one of three children who all took to music under the influence of their drummer father. Her first chosen instrument was the flute, with which she engaged in six years of private classical training before her attention turned to the world of percussion. With her father's drum set in the basement, Sue had instant access to an instrument and a tutor. Sue recalls,

> My dad had a trap set downstairs and he would show me the rudiments. I got into the Latin music and got myself a conga drum and I just started playing rock'n'roll, fusion and funk with the bands that were around. My older brother was a sax player, and he had a band, so he would use me for rehearsals; but when they went out for a gig, he'd leave me at home. But eventually my brother's band members ended up hiring me and I ended up playing gigs with them; that's how I got started. At first it was with the traps, but everybody would be like, 'where's the drummer? We're missing a drummer'. But the guys would point at me and say, 'she's the drummer!' You couldn't be a drummer as a woman, there was no work for that back then. The attitude was that women can't play hard like guys can, but I used to say, 'that's what microphones are for!' You don't always want bashing, personally I want a more dynamic sound, which women are great at. I used to think that they let women play percussion because they consider it colour and it didn't bother the rest of the guys in the band, the 'real musicians' – who didn't even want you there really. They tolerated you. But I soon started to get gigs with different people and then I got into the Latin field through tooling around with friends.

These days, Latin percussion has become a discipline of academic study, being taught in well-regarded institutions such as Berklee College of Music; however, when Sue discovered her love of rhythm, Latin percussion wasn't something you studied, it was something you felt. 'Back then you didn't learn Latin music in school. They didn't have that. You had to learn it by doing it. You played with the guys; they would just show you and you did it. But now you've got the Latin music guys teaching at colleges. But back then they didn't read music, it was all about the feel'. Sue isn't entirely unschooled, however. Having received a BA in Anthropology from Barnard College, she furthered her graduate studies at Mannes College of Music at night, endeavouring to earn her credentials in Music Theory, a subject that eluded her; not that this has hindered her ascension to the highest professional achievements in her field. Sue admits,

> I went to Mannes because I wanted to take some Theory and Ear Training and Dictation, but I could never really get Theory. I have a really good ear, so I could tell you whatever intervals I was hearing, but my problem with Theory and Dictation was that I never knew how to write out the chord. My teacher would say, 'there is no such chord!' I did take some mallet lessons; I took six months with Richard Brown of the Houston Symphony Orchestra after he had come up to New York for a little while. Six months is not enough for anything, but it was enough for me to get by, I discovered that the mallet instrument was for me the link between melody and percussion. When Joe Jackson wanted vibes or mallets, I memorized those parts. I'm kind of a jack of all trades as a percussionist. I'm old school, my favourite players are Tito Puente and Ray Barretto. But that style has changed; Tito's timbale playing was very syncopated, but if you look at the current generation of players, they do all these rudiments on the congas and timbales, they do a lot of double rolling when they do a solo. But I'm from way back, so I like to fill in the spaces with the bassline, but now it's all these rolls as fast as they can play, and I didn't learn that way. There was nothing written out back then; when we were doing it, you had garage bands who got together and learned to play together. The thing about percussion is it can be rhythm and it can be colour, though personally I'm a rhythm player, I like to be with the rhythm section. Although I don't often get a chance to play that way; usually if I'm going into the studio, I'm doing overdubs. But I like to be with the band, to play with the other musicians. I was never really into the colour thing; I do it, but I don't really like all that tinkly stuff, I want to be pounding on the timbales or the congas. With percussion you must decide upon what instrumentation because there's a load of stuff that you could play. It's not like flute, where all you are playing is flute. With percussion you could play this drum, that drum, or the triangle, the shakers, or whatever. You also have to decide what rhythm you want to use – what are you actually going to play to the music. And then where you want to place it in the song is another consideration. So, my talent or strong point is layering. I like that,

it's like a puzzle piece for me, you listen to a song on a demo that they give you and I create my parts.

Sue parlayed her talents into the busy, high-pressure world of recording sessions for commercials. For someone who could not sight-read music well, she was still able to provide the right rhythms for her time-sensitive, money-counting producers, meaning for a busy schedule but also for plenty of opportunities to feel insecure whilst being surrounded by topflight accredited studio players. Sue recalls,

I had some friends who had jingle houses and they wanted to use me all the time. But I didn't really read music; I only knew how to read flute music. I never learned how to read drum charts; I could just follow lead sheets. And you need to be able to read for jingles because it's intense, just between twenty and sixty seconds long and it's all weird time signatures, like 3/4 or 6/8, to make it fit into that. The session is all done in twenty minutes, and they usually only run the track three times. I just had a really good ear and a really good eye. I remember one time doing a Cleveland Plain Dealer commercial at Dick Lavsky's music house. Dick just loved me, and I worked with his wife, so he would hire me, but I always felt insecure because I wasn't out of that scene. I was never in any scene. Whenever I would arrive, I felt like an outsider. Everybody knew each other and so it was always that awkward situation where it felt like everybody's head would turn whenever I walked in. I'm sure that wasn't true but that's how it felt. So, I went in to do this jingle and I see it's a big room and there's a concert master, they've got strings and horns, they're putting out the charts, and my mouth is just going dry. I was playing the bongos and percussion. They had this other woman percussionist, Susan Evans, who played vibes and mallets, and everyone always used to think we were the same person – because there was only one Susan that could be a percussionist, right? But that's how it was back then! So, they kick off the song – it goes, 'When the news breaks…' and everybody is playing in half time except for the drums and the percussion, which were going top speed, but Grady Tate is drumming and is just over there cool grooving. So, we did one cut, and they then say, 'okay, cut out measures 24 and increase the tempo to four beats'. So, it got even faster! I was so freaked out, I had gum in my mouth that had just turned to wood; but I managed to do it. That is why I tell young people now to get their training.

Not one for remaining strictly studio bound, Sue soon became a founding member of the 14-piece all-female salsa act, Latin Fever. The band began as the brainchild of the wife of noted keyboardist, Larry Harlow. Celebrated as an innovator in the realm of Afro-Cuban music, Harlow worked closely with Fania Records, the New York-based label which specialized in salsa music. Harlow, along with the likes of Rubén Blades, Celia Cruz, Ray Barretto, and many more, were heavily promoted by Fania as part of their 'All Stars' stable which grew in popularity throughout the late 1960s and into the '70s. With most of Fania's roster of performers being male, Harlow wasn't convinced that there were enough female musicians around to form a successful group. His wife thought otherwise…

> Larry's wife, Rita, was looking to form a Latin band, she got all of us together and that's how it started. She rehearsed us. But it was a bet, basically – Larry told his wife that she wouldn't be able to get a band of women together that could play. But she did. Larry Harlow was the keyboard player for Fania Records, and he had his own band. We knew all those players and vocalists from Fania from when we were on that circuit. We would often be on the same bill. We did a Fania all-stars concert at Madison Square Garden twice – once with Latin Fever and Larry Harlow, and the second year I played a timbale solo with the vocalist Ismael Quintana and his group, and everyone went crazy. It was really good.

Despite Harlow's initial cynicism towards the idea of a successful all-female salsa band, he produced an album for the group which was released in 1978. Comprised of Latin, funk, and soul, the release entitled *Larry Harlow Presents Latin Fever* went to the top of the Latin charts and yielded a number one hit single, 'Lo Que Te Gusta Mas'.

> We had great arrangements from Larry, and his band came in and got us working as a section. We were also one of the first bands to perform bilingually, in Spanish and English. We debuted and it was a big hit. And then we went out on the road. We toured with that band for a year around '77/'78. That was my start in Latin music.

Sue's session career in the mainstream music world began in earnest when she received a call telling her she was to play on a record by the man who wrote some of the most popular and iconic American songs of the twentieth century. The person on the other end informed her that, 'you're going to do a session for this guy, he's a little black man named Otis Blackwell'. While the world has known the name Elvis Presley ever since Sam Phillips took notice of the unusual but intriguing sound coming out of his Sun Records recording booth, it took many years without due recognition before people would know the name Otis Blackwell. Without doubt, the man left a significant stamp on the American songbook, that which Elvis received most approbation for appropriating. Sue says,

> He wrote many huge hits for Elvis, 'Return to Sender', 'Don't Be Cruel' – and he is the voice of Elvis. Elvis stole his voice! And The Colonel took all his music. Otis probably got paid fifty dollars for songs which made millions. Later, he did get recognition by the Recording Academy, but before the 1950s they weren't getting royalties, but he did get money for it later on. So, I go down to the studio, which was on 48th Street, and the engineers are there, they tell me where to set up, and all these other people are coming in. Then I hear this voice which sounds exactly like Elvis, and I go, 'whoa!' He was doing the title song for a movie about Elvis which was called *The King of Rock & Roll*. He wrote it and he sang it, and then Elvis died right at that very time, so they shelved that project. But he came out from behind the booth, and he was this little, tiny, chubby black guy and he was terrific, a very nice, sweet man. We did a couple of cuts and that's what that situation was about. It was a studio session call, so the people who called me for that would call me for other stuff, but it didn't specifically function as a lead-in to other things.

Indeed, the gig that really did make people sit up and take notice and lead-in to a series of further high-profile work was the one that Sue got after that fateful trek downtown in the winter of 1982 to meet Joe Jackson. The Englishman had descended upon the cultural epicentre of New York City to soak up the sheer variety of multicultural art that the great metropolis can provide. In particular, the city's vibrant Latin musical culture proved influential to his writing and recording of his fifth studio album, *Night and Day*, and which would play right into Sue's wheelhouse. 'I love Latin music!' Sue enthuses. 'My major is Latin World Percussion. When Joe came to the city, he was going downtown to listen to all the Latin music and seeing all the Latin bands that were around. So, he was interested in bringing Latin flavours to that album, he wanted to do the sights and sounds of New York'. Ultimately, she was hired for the gig. Though it was a close one, as she recalls:

> When I answered the ad in *The Village Voice*, Joe's manager asked what my background in Latin music was, and I said, 'Latin Fever, Larry Harlow, Fania Records...' and he goes, 'okay, great. What else?' But I got called in to the rehearsal room and we did four songs from the record; they said, 'play whatever you want to play to them'. So, I did, and they liked it. But I wasn't familiar with Joe at all. To me, Joe Jackson is Michael Jackson's father. I went to the record store to pick up his stuff and familiarise myself with him.

> But me being an idiot, I'm looking in the 'J' racks like he's just some nobody. And then I see this Joe Jackson section and I discover he has like four albums already. That's when I started to get nervous.

Sue needn't have worried, her bona fides were impeccable, and evidently impressed Jackson.

> I was the last person to audition, they brought me in at the very end, and then they said, 'now we have a problem'. I asked what the problem is, and they said, 'well, we had somebody whom we thought we were going to be using, so now we are going to have to bring both of you back'. The other guy was Ricardo Torres who played bongos and some percussion on the record, and he was an excellent Latin player. But Joe does every type of music, and I was more well-rounded in the various styles of music and that's how I eventually got the gig. But they had pretty much given it to Ricardo before I came in. Joe let me put percussion on *Night and Day*, except for the mallet parts that he had, but otherwise all the percussion are my arrangements.

Night and Day was released to much acclaim in the summer of 1982 and peaked at number four on the Billboard Top 200 chart. The album became, and remains, the singer's biggest commercial success. It is a slick record of diverse musical styles and impeccable engineering, a credible pop statement for the discerning 1980s music aficionado as well as the casual radio listener; the perfect vehicle for the players to showcase their performances of class and style to musical peers and potential future collaborators. Sue went to work with Jackson on and off for the next three decades. So distinctive was her work with him, on his most notable albums and their respective tours, that Sue was often mistakenly perceived as exclusively Joe Jackson's percussionist.

> The thing about rock'n'roll and pop is it's like a gimmick – if you were going for an audition and they already had one woman in the band then that's it, you knew you weren't going to get called back to work with them because there was only room for one. One time I auditioned for an artist and got the gig, but all these guys were saying, 'oh, all you have to do is put on a dress and you can get the job'. Despite all the gigs the guys had, they were complaining because a woman got one lousy gig; they were freaking out saying, 'all they want is women percussionists'. That was always the way, but I have to say that working with Joe Jackson was the best thing that could ever have happened because he didn't care if you were a woman, a man, a cat, an alien – if you could play and do what he wanted you to do, that was fine. But working with Joe ended

up being kind of like the Rita Moreno story she told about winning the Oscar and then not working for another few years after that. Nobody knew what to do with her! It was similar in that I got all these accolades from *Night and Day* and everybody knew my name, all the recording people and everything, but I wasn't getting any calls for a little while; people thought I was 'Joe Jackson's percussionist'. That is the perception people have of you if you work with one person for too long.

Wisely seeing beyond that perception was one of the biggest acts of the moment: Simple Minds. The Scottish quintet were ensconced at Manhattan's Right Track Studios recording their seventh studio album, *Once Upon a Time* with producing powerhouses Jimmy Iovine and Bob Clearmountain. The album marked a notable shift in the band's sound, having abandoned the quirky new wave aesthetic of their previous efforts in favour of crafting the stadium-sized style that would become their trademark. Just as *Night and Day* had done for Joe Jackson, this album would bring Simple Minds to the masses and the airwaves. For the subsequent tour, the core band of Jim Kerr and co. would not be enough to fill out busy arrangements of the *Once Upon a Time* tracks on the massive stages on which they would appear across the world. Their ever-expanding sound called for a skilled percussionist, and thus the band evoked the name of Sue Hadjopoulos.

Simple Minds wanted me because I had worked with Joe Jackson, so they knew the record label, they knew me from *Night and Day* and the tour for that, but how they actually got me was because they were in the studio one day and they were asking if anyone knows who Sue Hadjopoulos is. They could have called the record company, but no, they just happened to be talking in the lounge and a friend of mine was working there as a studio manager and when they said, 'does anybody know where Sue Hadjopoulos is?' she goes, 'Are you looking for Sue Hadjopoulos? I have her number! She lives right down the block'. That is how they got in touch with me. Not from the record label or anything official like that, it's crazy how it works sometimes. Simple Minds were huge over in Europe but not in America. They finally made it to the States with 'Don't You (Forget About Me)' and that was brilliant because they decided to record here, and I lived in Midtown Manhattan West, so I was near all the studios. And that was an interesting situation; I got a phone call one day and it was Paul Kerr on the line. I wasn't familiar with Paul, but I answered it and he was like, 'Hi, this is Paul Kerr...' and he mentions Simple Minds. I'm writing it down, and I had some friends over who were overhearing me talking with Paul and they are getting all excited, like 'Simple Minds!' They tell me they are at the studio, Right Track, and asked me if I would be interested in coming in and laying down some percussion tracks. Jimmy Iovine and Bob Clearmountain were producing it and I said, 'yeah!' So, I did it and it was after that they asked me to be part of the band and do the tour. All the ways I've gotten these gigs have been very mystical and lucky. The subsequent tour was huge; it was mega. We went everywhere! I worked with them for a year. They were very nice. When I first started with them, I went over to London, and we rehearsed at the bass player's place. I couldn't understand a word they said, they had heavy Glasgow accents, and then they would use the lingo on top of that. So, we got together and rehearsed in one set place, and what was great about playing with the Minds, again as with Joe and Cyndi, I was the first percussionist to ever play with the group. There had never been any percussion on any of the songs, so it was purely my interpretation and my percussion arrangements. I was also lucky in that the people that I worked with would usually want to pair you up with another woman in the band then, like with Simple Minds. They had Robin Clark as a vocalist, and they used her on the record, and they used me on the record too, but they had already done the videos with her. This was the first time Simple Minds used other people and they wanted us to be part of the group, we were part of Simple Minds.

Going for a hat trick of major world tours within the first half of the 1980s, Sue would hit the road with one of the true breakout stars of the MTV era: Cyndi Lauper. Having blazed a trail with the vibrant party pop and synth-based balladry of her debut album, *She's So Unusual* (1983), Lauper continued in much the same vein with her 1986 sophomore record, *True Colors*. Sue initially met Lauper whilst on a short tour with 'Lovergirl' singer Teena Marie. Taking Lauper's visit as a choice moment to make connections and network, Sue asked the pop star if she could send her some material for future consideration, to which Lauper agreed. And so when Lauper was preparing to mount a massive tour in support of *True Colors* an opportunity arose for Sue to showcase her talents within the mainstream pop world. The ensuing tour, which was Lauper's first headlining global trek, spread across North America, Europe, Australia, and Asia throughout 1986 and 1987.

I was always freelance, and I would be contracted by a band for a year, that's how it was with Simple Minds and Joe Jackson for example. My first major tour went on for over a year, and I didn't realize until after that most tours only go out for a month or six weeks. The first three big tours I did were long world tours, and it was only after those that I saw how it usually happens. Cyndi Lauper was another of those big ones and the audition for that was kind of synchronous. I had sent my resume to her office after meeting her on the Teena Marie tour and then I heard from some people in New York that Cyndi was getting ready to go out on tour and she's looking for a percussionist who sings and I was like, 'I want to go!' Even though I had never really sung professionally I said, 'okay, let me do this!' A friend of mine lost out on that gig because she said she couldn't sing, so I try to say 'yes' to everything unless I think I'm really going to mess up. I got in on the audition and Cyndi says, 'we're well aware of your percussion talent but we want to see how well you can sing'. So, we start playing 'What's Going On', which was going to be a single coming out and the video that we were all in, and she starts singing 'Mother, mother...' and then she points at me and says, 'take it!' and I just started singing. I figured she just liked my scrawny, scratchy voice, but in all fairness, we did have a good blend in terms of timbre. She did show me a lot of stuff. Cyndi Lauper was like my first vocal coach! How do you like that? And then I studied vocals with Katie Agresta, who is Cyndi's vocal coach, everybody has worked with Katie, even Joe Jackson! Cyndi got me in to see Katie. So, I sang with Cyndi. I never sang solo with Joe because the timbre is completely different, although I did sing background on '19 Forever'. I had enough to do on percussion anyway. Joy Askew was there with Joe and she was completely masterful. And they also had Mindy Jostyn, who has since passed.

While working with the pop dynamo led to many music industry eyes witnessing Sue's dual skills of percussion and singing, and thus more calls of employment, it also led to some unfortunate typecasting from those who should have known better. Sue recalls,

While I was with Simple Minds, I had decided to dye my hair a shade of blue. It wasn't an outrageous B-52s sartorial thing, but just a bit of a blue tinge which went well with Cyndi's kooky style. But that then led to typecasting and being misperceived. It came up when I got a call from the manager of this country artist who wanted me for some East Coast dates. I said, 'yeah, I'll do it' and then he goes, 'okay, but this is not a Cyndi Lauper type thing with blue hair'. I replied, 'Sir, I am a side musician. I do what I need to do for the particular act that I am working with. I will wear black if that's the thing'. I don't even know why he called me because he eventually decided that I wasn't right. He shouldn't have called me in the first place. I'm surprised that music industry people would typecast you, because they should know that being a side musician inherently means playing with lots of different people. But I eventually started getting calls again.

Despite a resume that would suggest apparent ease in obtaining place-
ments with successful musical acts, Sue has faced her fair share of resentment
for her choice to remain financially and legally conscious in an industry that
almost punishes you for doing so, as Sue describes:

> I had a friend who was an attorney, and whose services I would use,
> but they don't like musicians who have attorneys. They don't like
> that at all. One thing that always became a problem was that you
> would get paid for the tour, but as things would go on you might
> do a recording within that time, or they might record a show, and
> they would always say that is included in what you are being paid
> for. But one of the things that I insisted upon was a 'Grey Area
> Clause' which dictated that the salary was to do with playing live
> only; everything else has to be renegotiated, including any videos
> filmed or recordings made during this period. You can't do that
> now because everything is immediately recorded on cell phones
> and put on YouTube. It would be really annoying when you would
> get to the gig and then you see a 24-track mobile unit sitting out-
> side that they didn't tell you about. Everybody would bitch and
> moan, but guess who ended up the bad guy? They'd all say, 'yeah,
> let's complain', and then I'm the one sticking out there like a sore
> thumb.

Sue continues,

> I probably could have worked with more people, but there were
> several reasons why I didn't: one, being a single woman, it had to
> be on the level; and two, I wasn't going to be flying out anywhere
> without having it be secure. Then there are other reasons for not
> taking certain gigs, being that it would have been out of my own
> pocket, or because I felt it wouldn't have been a great experience.
> I've had some very last-minute down-to-the-wire calls, where you
> are supposed to be leaving on tour in two days and they still haven't
> agreed to contractual things. One example of that was when I got
> a call from Joe's producer asking me if I would be interested in
> working with Grace Jones on a record. I said, 'yeah, sure!' and he
> said, 'okay, I'll have them call you'. So, I get this call from this sec-
> retary who says, 'I have you booked on a flight to Compass Point,
> Bahamas...' and I'm like, 'whoa, wait a minute! What are you talking
> about?' I need to know some things first. So, I ask her, 'How many
> songs is it? Where is it? Do I need to bring equipment? Do you
> have equipment down there?' And she just goes, 'I don't know'. All
> these record company people act like they've never booked a trip
> before. Ever! And they always act like they didn't know there was

a contract. Eventually, this secretary says, 'I'll have Chris call you'. Chris Blackwell! The founder of Island Records. So, he called me on the phone, and I have to say it was ridiculous. He sounded like he had smoked something very strong. He goes, 'So yeah, what's the problem?' And I replied, 'I'm trying to find out what I'll be doing on this gig. What songs am I doing, and what are you paying me? Is it scale or what?' And he asks me, 'What's scale?' I'm there thinking this is all just going downhill fast. I ask him if I need equipment, and he says, 'Why? Don't you have any?' And I say, 'Yes, I have tons of equipment, but can I bring it, or what the heck?' So, we just tee-tered out and I knew that was it. Forget it. The end. After that, I found out that a couple of people who did play on the record said they didn't get paid, and they didn't get credit on it. So, here's the thing: if you're not going to get paid and you're not going to get credit, why the hell should you do it? So that you can tell people that you did it? Now, I love Grace Jones, I think she is phenomenal, I love 'Slave to the Rhythm' and all those songs that she did, but it was not for me to work with her. I can't, as a single woman, be traipsing down to Compass Point, Bahamas, not knowing what the hell is going on. I've turned down gigs because I knew it would be that kind of situation.

With Sue's profile increasing due to her work with major artists from both the mainstream and alternative worlds, it proved tricky when negotiating her fees, leading to missed opportunities for both Sue and the artists who wanted to work with her. Sue reveals,

It wasn't to do with being an expensive player, because the thing with that is it's always negotiable. It is not always up and up and up, it depends on how much they need you, and that was always a very fine line. Percussionists are always last to be hired and first to be fired. They would often call me after the fact; the record would be done, and I would go in for the sweetening session. I do like playing with the bands, although I have to say if I go in by myself then I know I can be fast. And to them, time is money. I would quote a certain amount, knowing what I could do in a certain time limit. One guy wanted to use me on something but said I was too expensive, so he ended up getting another Latin player who I know. Then a couple of weeks later he called me back and said, 'we'd like to hire you now'. He didn't know that I had talked with the engineer, who had told me who they hired instead of me. But I knew who it was, and this player was a very good Latin percussionist, so I was surprised it was a bomb. Latin can't always cross over to the pop or rock genres; it just doesn't sound right. I would say that I play

Latin pop or Latin rock; I can play the rhythms, but I make them sound rocky. Ultimately, they ended up paying for two people to do the session because they couldn't use the other player's parts on the final track.

Sue details further instances of the unfortunate reality of touring life, the side that concertgoers and industry outsiders are rarely privy to.

I have done a bit of touring with Rickie Lee Jones who is an amazing writer and performer. I would probably eliminate myself from gigs because I would just want to hear her play piano and sing. I'd be thinking, 'you don't need percussion on this song,' but I didn't say that. But why do all artists have to be so nutty?! She was a little bit crazy. When we were in Paris one time, she got mad when she was asked to do something or other, and so she left and went to England, leaving the band behind in Paris for a week. Needless to say, we had a blast!! Then she tried to get us to pay for our hotel rooms. I was like, 'What?! We're available to play!' I had to get on the phone to my attorney. It was like that with Teena Marie; she had a voice that was incredible, the band was superb, but the business end of it was very shady. It was the kind of gig where I wanted to make sure I got my ticket, and I left. They ended up owing me money and I did get the union involved. I'm very grateful to the AFM [American Federation of Musicians] because most of these things were not done through the union, they were just contract with the artist; that's mainly the way it was back then, whereas nowadays it's mostly through the AFM. Another time I had to call them was back in the jingle days. I was called in to play percussion on something, so I went to play on maybe three segments, for Pringles and whatever else. Some time went by, and I was waiting to get paid for it, so I called them up and ask what's up with that. They go, 'oh, that was just a demo, it didn't go final, and we don't pay for that.' I said, 'no, I don't work for free. That's ridiculous!' So, I called the AFM, and they got me my money. But they do tell you that if you fight this then you're not going to get work with those people anymore. I said, 'fine, if they're not going to pay me, why would I want to work with them anyway?'

The 1980s had been a prolific time for Sue, having recorded and toured the world several times with some of the biggest artists of the decade. She capped the decade with respective appearances on the 1989 releases of two performers of extremely contrasting aesthetic sensibilities: performance artist Laurie Anderson's fifth studio recording *Strange Angels* and former Hanoi Rocks frontman Michael Monroe's second solo work *Not Fakin' It*. Anderson's

Strange Angels was perhaps her least esoteric and indeed most musical album to date. Drawing in some of the most well-regarded artists around, the album includes performances from the likes of Arto Lindsay, Anton Fier, Tony Levin, and Mike Thorne. The mammoth production effort saw Sue being brought in as one of many percussionists contributing to the album's complex arrangements. Going into the 1990s, Sue continued to work with an ever-diverse range of artists, including session work for former Talking Heads frontman David Byrne's self-titled fourth solo record (1994), the sixth release of Brooklyn alt-rock duo They Might Be Giants (*Factory Showroom*, 1996), and the chart-topping English language self-titled debut of Puerto Rican pop star, Ricky Martin (1999).

'I wasn't familiar with They Might Be Giants', Sue admits.

> These guys were coming from rock, and I wasn't that familiar with rock'n'roll, so I had to run out and buy all their records to acquaint myself with them. I wouldn't stress too much, but I wanted to know what their groove was. I always had to do my research. When they called me, they were doing this song called 'S-E-X-X-Y' which was this throwback to the funk thing. I was always into funk and fusion, so that was tremendous fun. I was more familiar with David Byrne, thanks to Talking Heads and all that. Susan Rogers was recording it and it was great having a female producer, though I have to say that was a bit of an uncomfortable situation, it wasn't an easy session. David's style is so different, and he wasn't there the whole time. They used a lot of percussionists on that album, there were some playing on different songs and then four percussionists all playing together on one song. I always try and write down what I did so I can remember. I can usually tell if it's me, but other times I can't. Sometimes they'll say, 'we really love what you did!' but then you listen to it, and you go, 'where is it? I don't hear anything!' Joe Jackson is the only one who ever put me up in the mix level with the drums. He has the snare and congas level. Usually when you're a percussionist you're in the background, you're off to the side... except for Joe! Ricky Martin was a weird session too. He wasn't there, he was in Puerto Rico. He called in and I talked to him. They wanted to re-do a song that they had already done on a previous album but in a different style, so they called in more rock players to give it a different sound. They drove us up to Woodstock because by the time they decided to do it everywhere in the city was already booked. So, they picked us up and drove us all the way up to Woodstock and we were there recording various versions of the song until the early hours. Everyone was flying in from LA and all over the place, and he was calling in on the phone. These people came in, did their thing, and took off while we were still there

packing up. We got back to the city in the morning. They ultimately decided to use the first take of the recording we did when we first got there! It was a crazy 24-hour session.

Sue continued to juggle her recording work with further touring commitments with an ever-expanding range of artists, embarking on national and international jaunts with the likes of Kenny Loggins, Clarence Clemons, and Enrique Iglesias. One memorable moment of her 1990s touring times was when she entered the joyously kitsch realm of The B-52s for their 1992 Interdimensional Tourgasm trek around the States. This tour was particularly notable for featuring vocalist Julee Cruise, who was then known for her dream pop solo album *Floating into the Night* (1989) and her significant contribution to the hugely successful *Twin Peaks* soundtrack. Cruise became a B when she replaced original member Cindy Wilson. Sue and Julee would soon become firm friends and future collaborators. Sue recalls,

> Julee was so crazy. We used to go out and she would make me laugh. I worked on a song with Julee called 'Never Again'. I showed her this instrumental part that I had done which was very much in her style of music, so she added lyrics to it. It was a really great time with a good group of people. And what a party they were! It was just a fun band to be part of. They're not musically trained, except Kate who is, but they came along and created this sound that is incredible and so distinctive. And then they went on to have so many hits! But I loved The B-52s because they were gay and they were women; when there's a lot of guys, it can be too much testosterone to be around for a woman. It's like, 'please, give me a shot of oestrogen'. A lot of the time they don't have the finer things for women, such as tissues, a mirror... the nice things. Because guys don't put makeup on, so they don't consider those things. But everybody in The B-52s was putting makeup on!

While Sue's work has been most visible while performing across the world's concert stages throughout the last four decades, her repertoire has also extended to the theatre world. Sue has worked on shows such as *Behind the Beat*, a 1999 musical autobiography of 1970s disco queen Vicki Sue Robinson, and the 2008 debut re-staging of playwright Jason Robert Brown's *Songs for a New World*, directed by Debbie Slevin. This was the first approved performance by Brown for this show. He allowed Slevin liberty in staging, music, and percussion; in fact, Brown had been aware and complimentary of Sue's work with Joe Jackson. *Night and Day* strikes again! While Sue is particularly fond of some of those theatrical moments, other efforts are lamented upon in hindsight with a soupçon of regret.

I have said 'yes' to doing things that I shouldn't have, and one of those was an Off-Broadway show that turned out to be horrible. I made a mess of it. But in all fairness, it was because I was trying to be a sub for a guy who was six feet tall, and you can't change the setup in the pit, plus there was some more intricate mallet work on it and I can't read that. But I said I would do it; I tried to learn it and memorize it, but it was a disaster. Not because of the music, but because it was out of sorts; I had to be up on a pedestal to try and play and I could hardly reach all the percussion, so I wasn't comfortable. I tried it, but it wasn't my thing.

The physical predicament that Sue faced is shared by many women drummers or players of large instruments: height challenges.

I am only 4'11' so I am handicapped by even having a jam playing with other guy musicians. I can't even reach the top of the congas or get good grip on the timbales when they are set up for a normal sized guy. That's why I had to do my own thing and do shows where I started from the ground up as the originator of the part, so it was MY setup. It is another reason why subbing gigs for me is not generally an option.

Other shows have remained particularly dear to the musician, notably her work with composer-social activist Bernice Reagon and her daughter Toshi Reagon. Joining the mother-daughter duo for the premiere performance of Flaubert's *The Temptation of Saint Anthony* at Ruhr Triennale Festival in Duisburg, Germany, directed by Robert Wilson, Sue recalls 'a fascinating show where I got to create some truly interesting parts. An amazing experience'. Along with author-composer Rosa Soy, she was responsible for a children's musical entitled *The Rose Slippers*, based on a poem by Cuban patriot and philosopher José Martí, 'Los Zapaticos de Rosa'. Sue co-wrote the Latin-infused music and libretto as well as creating the sound design for the show which premiered Off-Off-Broadway in 1998.

'It was done Off-Off-Broadway, actually Off-Off-Off', Sue confirms.

It got a cute little review in *The New York Times* and won a Jackie White National Children's Theatre award. We still have it; it's written as a book and a musical play, but it would really have to be developed. We took it to ASCAP [American Society of Composers, Authors and Publishers] for a class on libretto and song writing. We sent it to regional theatres and publishers. It was interesting to see their criticisms which made us laugh. Some said you can't have a ghost narrator character, for example. Isn't that what Shakespeare did? Ha. Some said you can't have animal and insect characters that talk to the human little girl character. Isn't that what Disney does? To get into this industry you really have to know people and be connected to get into those kinds of places. Ultimately, it's not really my style, it's more of my co-writer Rosa's kind of thing. But it was an interesting exercise to develop something in a new medium and work on it, it was a new learning experience in doing something different.

Forty years after answering that anonymous notice in *The Village Voice* which led to a lauded and prolific career on the road and on record, Sue Hadjopoulos contemplates the key to her longevity in an industry that doesn't make it easy for any woman, let alone one who walks to the beat of her own bongos. And one who operates on a resolve of independence, shrewdness, and unwillingness to unquestioningly take the bullshit that women are expected to comply with in the name of perceived accomplishment.

The success that I've had is because I wasn't really familiar with most of the artists that I worked with. Everything I've done, I had no knowledge of it beforehand, so therefore I didn't have a chance to be overwhelmed and freaked out about who it was. That has been an advantage. I've played with a lot of artists, and my approach to each gig has always come from life experience. Latin music is very intricate, but my education was through practical experience and performing. While I've had some formal training, it is my background of just playing with people that has served me best. I hear the song and I hear the mood of it; that's what inspires how I play and what I play. When I look back at it now, observing all the work that I've done, I think, 'how did I do all of that?!' I've been the luckiest person in the world.

Postscript

Wayne Byrne

Over the course of a year, Amanda and I set out to document the careers of ten musicians of industry renown. They run the gamut of genres from punk to pop, from classical to jazz, and everything in-between. We conceived of this book without any mission statement or ideological rhetoric. In an era when anybody's personal viewpoint can be (mis)taken for political philosophy, we would be loath for this book to be taken for anything other than a narrative on that which the author of our foreword, Jennifer Finch, writes are 'ten lives well lived'. Amanda and I began the process of research by interviewing each woman we chose to profile, beginning with Joy Askew. Our conversation with Joy was just that: an intimate, informal discussion. That set the template for all our interviews, with Amanda taking the lead in bringing us back to the origins of each subject, to trace the inspiration and education that led to a life on the road as a professional musician. Some names appear across several chapters as experiences are shared within certain bands and social circles, but every story told is uniquely theirs. Each is a tale of talent developed with discipline and dedication, whether academic or autodidactic; we provided a canvas for these artists to detail how their distinctive approach to the craft and subsequent career was informed by time, place, family, and other personal factors.

In charting and illustrating each of these unique paths as we did, future generations of female musicians can learn from these ladies' lives. Without deliberate endeavour to make the book a cautionary tale, the inherent intimacies of the conversations revealed a vulnerable side to perceived success. In documenting the road to professional achievement and acclaim, home truths about the realities of a peripatetic life on the road emerged. That with success comes sacrifice, but that is the price that any artist will pay for their passion.

These women are not in the habit of giving interviews and speaking about themselves. By the very nature of their work, they are there to support the music in the moment while remaining in relative anonymity working in the shadows of a frontperson. Their role is to bring skill, not ego. But their tale is worth telling, and it is only through mutual admiration or pre-existing friendships between Amanda and these women that such candid conversations could occur. It was an honour for me to be there and to help bring it to literary fruition; to catalogue these conversations, set them in temporal and social contexts, and make available these stories to students, teachers, readers, writers, musicians … a tangible historical record of how those ten lives were lived.

www.ingramcontent.com/pod-product-compliance
Lightning Source LLC
Chambersburg PA
CBHW040408110426
42812CB00011B/2485